IT'S AN OLD
CALIFORNIA CUSTOM

It's an Old California Custom

LEE SHIPPEY

THE VANGUARD PRESS, INC. · NEW YORK

The early California illustrations on the title page and on pages 27, 201, and 265 are from The Bettmann Archive; those on pages 49, 157, and 185 are reproduced from Clarence P. Hornung's *Handbook of Early American Advertising Art*; those on pages 68 and 134 are from Culver Service; the illustration on page 248 was adapted from a drawing by Charles Nahl in *Old Block's Sketch Book*.

Designed by Stefan Salter
Manufactured in the United States of America by H. Wolff,
New York, N. Y.

TO MY HELPSPEND

my companion in ten thousand happy adventures, vicarious and personal—vicarious in the good books we have read together, actual in the many trips we have taken together in quest of human interest. She is my comrade in nearly all I read and write, and she read aloud all or part of nearly a hundred books while I took notes for this one.

ACKNOWLEDGMENTS

In compiling data for this book I have been generously aided by friends who are veritable geysers of knowledge: Vierling Kersey, for whom I wrote a book while he was State Superintendent of Public Instruction; Lindley Bynum, assistant to the president of the University of California; Roger Starrett, president of the Historical Society of Southern California; Mrs. Guy Giffen, librarian for the Pioneer Society of San Francisco; Ana Begue de Packman, author of *Leather Dollars* and *Early California Hospitality*. W. W. Robinson, Robert J. Woods, J. Gregg Layne, and Roger Dalton aided personally; and I am indebted to the Bancroft Library, the Wells-Fargo Library, and the Los Angeles Public Library. Many of the illustrations are made from historic prints in the Huntington Library. Scores of source books were read, but the ones directly quoted have been acknowledged in the text.

L.S.

CONTENTS

IT'S AN OLD
CALIFORNIA CUSTOM

TO RIDE FORTH SEEKING
ROMANCE

Ι T TOOK all the other states and nearly all the other countries to make California. Its builders have come from all quarters of the globe. It has been under five flags, and if a bank of fog had not kept Sir Francis Drake from finding the Golden Gate, or if Bouchard, French pirate carrying letters of marque from Argentina, had chosen to raise another flag or two after capturing its capital, it would have been under more. It is big enough to be a nation and has five distinct climates. And those who led every wave of migration into it were daring adventurers. Thus it has inherited the customs of many lands but has modified all of them to its own personality. For many generations it was so far from its rulers—first those in Spain, then those in Mexico, then those in Washington—it was a law unto itself, and Californians developed a spirit of arrogant independence.

From its beginnings as a unit, California developed traits which had not been possible anywhere else. In a land in which grazing livestock could find pasturage all the year and needed no stables, and where there was so much land there was no need for fences, and anyone who had land could get all the Indians he needed, on slavery terms, to do all the hard work, and horses, cattle, and sheep multiplied so that a rancher didn't know or really care whether he had twenty thousand head of cattle or a mere fifteen thousand, seven thousand head of horses or a mere five thousand, it was natural for such easy-going habits and such grandiose hospitality to spring up as the world had probably never witnessed before.

Yet California's beginnings were so hard and poverty-stricken that soldiers and missionaries sent to it felt they were being banished to a benighted wilderness, and many of the first settlers had to be recruited from jails. But soon it became a land of fabulous abundance and developed a casualness about property lines which continued into the days of United States ownership. It didn't bother about surveyors. When property was sold or given away the measurements were made by two horsemen with a *reata*. One would ride forward till the *reata* was taut, then halt his horse, and the other would ride forward till it was taut again. If a fly bit a horse and it moved a few feet, or if a wet *reata* was stretched a few feet longer than its supposed length, it made no difference. A few acres made no difference. As late as 1870, there was not a fence between Los Angeles and San Francisco except in towns or around gardens and orchards, to keep out deer and livestock.

For more than two centuries after Cabrillo claimed California for Spain in 1542, it was not considered worth worrying about. But in 1741 Bering and Churikof, sent by the Czar, made their way to Alaska and established a trading post at Sitka. It took a long time for news of that to get to Spain, but it aroused worry when it got there. Spain didn't want California but didn't want Russia to have it. It was decided to establish missions in California, with soldiers to guard them. The idea was that the padres would Christianize the Indians and make it safe for settlers to enter the wilderness.

[5]

The first mission was established in San Diego in 1769, and from it Portolá's expedition meandered up the coast. Though the occupation was inspired by politics, the padres were zealous. The Indians were friendly and docile and came in droves to be baptized. It was an easy way to get gaudy beads and tidbits of strange foods. Though some of them did exquisite basket weaving, and their pottery had almost been refined into porcelain, the Indians were childishly delighted with the baubles the white men brought. Later, when they found they had to obey the white men's rules and do menial work for them, many of them rebelled. But it is doubtful if the aborigines of any other part of America were benefited as much by their conquerors. Previously, they had known nothing of agriculture, but relied on nuts, acorns, berries, grasshoppers, snakes, and game for food, and there were seasons when they starved. Portolá's expedition brought two hundred cattle and six remount horses for every soldier, and it was to admire those wonders as well as to see the strange men with white faces that Indians came by thousands to be baptized. They were taught so much of agriculture and animal husbandry as to banish hunger for everyone throughout California's pastoral era.

Soon a chain of missions stretched along four hundred miles of the California coast, each pre-

empting vast areas. At first the soldiers who
guarded those missions yearned only to be allowed
to go back to God's country and never see California again. But once the Indians were taught
to build and farm, some soldiers realized that in
California they might live in such ease and spa-
ciousness as princes might envy. So in 1784, according to W. W. Robinson's *Ranchos Become Cities*,
three veterans who felt they had earned the right
petitioned Governor Fages to grant them land, and
the Governor generously agreed. Why not, as no
one was being robbed except the Indians? Those
grants, all in what later became Los Angeles
County, were roughly thirty miles square, but, as
their boundaries were the sea, water courses, and
the mountains, some were bigger.

The example set by those three veterans was
quickly followed by others at San Diego, Santa
Barbara, and Monterey, and soon the coast was
lined by some fourteen vast estates, they and the
mission lands taking up practically all of it for well
over three hundred miles.

The simplest adobe huts were erected on those
ranches at first. But workers were so plentiful and
cheap, and prosperity and herds increased at such a
rate, that the grantees vigorously set to work to
populate the land. Families of twenty or more became common, and the average number of children

per couple was about twelve. Bayard Taylor tells
that one Californian was pointed out to him who
was the father of thirty-six, and it is recorded that
José Maria Martin Ortega was one of a family of
twenty-one children and was himself the father
of that number. Señora José Castro was the mother
of twenty-six. An ever increasing number of
mestizos, whose fathers were the original unknown
soldiers, were scattered about the landscape, too.
When the Hijar colonists reached San Juan Bau-
tista, after an overland journey of many months
from Mexico, a cart was overturned, and when it
was righted it was found that two brand-new
colonists had been added to the party.

With hundreds of retainers to do the work and
thousands of fine horses to ride, it was natural for
those early settlers to go a-riding. There was not
an inn in the land, but every house was a free inn.
Families living thirty miles or more from their
nearest neighbors were glad to see company. If
one was a person of quality his visit would be made
the excuse for a *baile,* which rarely lasted less than
two days and often lasted a week or two. Then, too,
the man with twenty children, or even only sixteen or twelve, was likely to have some lovely
daughters. So fathers went a-riding to look for suitable brides for their sons, and young men, as soon
as they could get their fathers' consent, went a-

riding too. All marriages were arranged by the elders, and girls were at such a premium it was the obligation of the bridegroom's family to supply the dowry and all the wedding finery.

No youth could go a-riding without his father's consent—he could not even shave without it. And that consent rarely was given before the youth was twenty-two, which was considered the proper age for marriage—for a man. Girls married at thirteen or fourteen. But the young men could see the girls, show off before them, dance with them, and accompany them on *mariendas,* or picnics. We have Bancroft's word for it that "each horseman carried a fair one before him on his saddle when they went to a *marienda,*" and after they had gathered flowers or berries in the woods there was always music, dancing, and singing, which usually lasted nearly all night. It was a dull caballero who couldn't exchange a few tender words and even keepsakes with the girl of his choice on such occasions, and when he got home he could find some helpful relative who would suggest to his father that that was the girl he should marry. Father was an absolute tyrant, but there have always been ways of influencing tyrants.

William Heath Davis, one of the first *gringos* to marry into California, wrote that young persons engaged to be married were scarcely allowed to see each other except in the presence of their parents. "If the suitor was considered a worthy person by the young lady's father, the young lady was communicated with"—but probably that wasn't often a great surprise to her. After that "a request in writing came from the young man to the father. If the application was considered satisfactory, there was a written reply."

To modern youth, that might look like a long way around, but it doesn't seem to have kept the young Californians of those days from having a good deal of fun. One of California's historic stories tells that when Padre de la Pena heard Don Pablo Sepulveda make a wager with Don Pio Pico that he would win the hearts of a dozen señoritas while making his tour of California, the padre set out to "ride and spread the alarm," leaving San Diego a day ahead of Don Pablo. Thus, when the gay caballero rode up to a rancho, he was welcomed with all courtesy, but his visit was not made the occasion for *bailes* or *mariendas*. He got little chance to see the señoritas, and when he met them they were cool and tantalizing, which was a painful shock to the young man's vanity. He rode a thousand miles and stopped at many places, but had no conquests to boast when he got home.

All that riding forth on the part of both parents and young men resulted in so many marriages that soon all the land-grant families of California were related. They formed a sort of aristocracy, a landed gentry class, and, as all of them had large families and vast acreages, the result was more ranchos and more relatives. A couple of years before Irvin S. Cobb died, he and his good friend Leo Carrillo, descendant of practically all the first families, took a trip through California together, and wherever they stopped Leo was busy introducing Irvin to his cousins. At last Cobb asked:

"Leo, do you mean to say all these people are really your cousins?"

"Certainly," said Carrillo. "You see, we all had the same ancestors. The Carrillos, the De la Guerras, the Bandinis, the Arguellos, and a lot more all intermarried."

"No doubt you're mighty proud of your ancestry," said Cobb, "but at least one of your ancestors must have been an Albemarle Sound shad."

One result of those marriages was that the habitual dress of all the women was black. It was the custom to wear mourning for a year for any close and honored relative, and, though the women could wear bright colors on festive occasions, they felt they had to wear black all the rest of the time. The men, who were the gaudy dressers of that period, merely wore crepe arm-bands.

Perhaps the best proof that plenty of love-making

went on despite parental tyranny lies in the fact
that many *gringos*, or outlanders, whom the Californians were forbidden even to know, married
some of the loveliest—and richest—señoritas, and
the most treasured stories of the pastoral era are the
tales of those romances.

Spain was so suspicious of countries that might
be land-hungry that trading with foreigners was
prohibited, but one of the oldest of California's customs is that of winking at laws it does not like. In
all the land there was not a store of any kind, and
it was only when a ship arrived that anything
could be bought or sold. Herds of deer and elk were
so numerous it was profitable to slaughter them for
their hides and tallow. Elk also were lassoed for
sport, because of their strength and fighting spirit,
as the Spaniards did not care for their meat. Herds
of cattle increased to such vast numbers that, when
a ship came in seeking hides and tallow, cattle
were slaughtered by thousands and only the
choicest portions of the meat were saved, the rest
being left for dogs or crows. The average rancher
needed from forty to sixty dogs to act as scavengers
about his home, while every village had a thousand. The unwritten law, according to Salvador
Vallejo, was that any hungry traveler might kill a
bullock, provided he hung the hide where coyotes

could not get it and the owner would see it. The meat was valueless, but hides were money.

When a ship was sighted, great bonfires were lit, partly to guide it and partly to notify ranchers for miles around, and the ranchers poured into town, no matter what ship it was. Signal Hill, in Long Beach, got its name from that custom. New England shoemakers became dependent on California hides, and Yankee clippers came around the Horn for them but ran up the Hawaiian flag when near California, entering its ports under false colors. The Californians knew they weren't Hawaiians, but they were in such need of cloth and sugar and merchandise of all kinds that they would have welcomed the devil himself, and even the good padres were compelled by necessity to trade with these foreigners.

In 1805, the Russian fur-trading colony at Sitka, Alaska, was dying out from starvation and scurvy. The Czar sent his chamberlain, Nikolai Petrovich Rezanov, to Sitka to see what could be done about it. Rezanov found the colony in a sad plight, with only enough food to last a few weeks, and felt that the only thing to do about it was to go to California, the land of plenty, in quest of food. An American ship, the "Juno," put in at Sitka, and Governor Baranof purchased its entire cargo, but all it could spare was not enough. When it sailed south for

Yerba Buena, as San Francisco was then named, Rezanov went with it, taking a cargo of furs.

Because of the hostility of the Spaniards, the Russians previously had traded with Indians north of Yerba Buena. But the "Juno" sailed into the little Spanish port. Alvarez Luis Arguello, son of the *commandante*, José Arguello, went out to meet the strange craft, but the little fort had its guns trained on it, or more or less at it, just the same.

It was hard for the Californians not to be hospitable, even to their enemies. Rezanov must have been a dashing fellow, and once the Spaniards were convinced his mission was friendly, he was entertained. The Spaniards would not trade with him. Their attitude was one of polite discouragement. It broke their hearts to refuse their guests anything, but their own needs were so great the law forbade exports. They wanted the Russians to return to Sitka with the conviction that California could do nothing for them.

However, with visitors in port it was customary to have a *baile*. So there was a little impromptu dance lasting three or four days, and the Russian nobleman met Concepcion Arguello, daughter of the *commandante*. Señoritas very often prefer blonds. What was the law of Spain in this faraway country, anyway? And what was the traditional submission to parental wishes, between friends? Concepcion became sorry for the poor, starving Russians, when California had so much more than it could eat. So, after a visit of many months, Rezanov not only got a shipload of provisions to take back to Sitka but sailed away with the plighted troth of the lovely Concepcion.

But Rezanov was said to be related to the Czar and could not marry without the Czar's consent. He sailed back to get that consent, and Concepcion waited for him for five years. Then, in 1811, the Russians returned, establishing a settlement at Rossiya, or Little Russia, only a day's march north of Yerba Buena, where they had traded before. They were headed by a man named Kuskof, who brought word that Rezanov had died in the wastes of Siberia without ever getting back to see the Czar. Concepcion entered a convent and was abbess at Benicia when she died. The still-popular California song "La Golondrina" is said to have been inspired by her sad romance, though it was written in Mexico afterward.

There is a postscript to the story of Rezanov and Concepcion. When the Russians returned to Rossiya, now known as Fort Ross, in 1811, they acquired rights by purchase from the Indians. That is, they gave the Indians three blankets, three pairs of breeches, two axes, and three hoes for a townsite and "the tillable land around it," perhaps ten thousand acres. Then a new governor came to Rossiya with a beautiful wife, said by some historians to have been "the first lady brought to California." At least she was the first to come direct from Europe and a court, wearing clothes which were not a year behind the styles. Her mere appearance on the scene seems to have changed the Spanish attitude. There were *bailes* and *mariendas* in her honor, and much visiting to and fro between Yerba Buena and Rossiya. That resulted in another complication. The Indians between Yerba Buena and Rossiya were brave and warlike, and their leader, Chief Solano, was a big and powerful man physically and figuratively. The Spaniards had finally won his friendship, and he, too, was an honored guest in Yerba Buena. When he saw the beautiful Russian, he wanted her for his squaw, and it was his habit to take whatever he wanted. He had laid plans for ambushing the Russians and carrying off the lovely visitor when the Spanish *commandante* heard of it and convinced Solano it was the wrong thing to do, as all the arms and power of Russia would be sent to avenge and punish, and all Solano's people would be killed or driven away.

This book is no history, but one cannot but speculate on what might have happened if Rezanov had come back and married the lovely daughter of the Spanish *commandante*, or if the Czar had felt it his duty to send a punitive expedition into an area so weakly held that a pirate from the far-off Argentine could sweep into its capital and sack several of its richest settlements. It was only ten years after the beautiful Russian came to Rossiya that New Spain successfully revolted against Old Spain, and California was not very friendly to the successful revolt. The first famiiles had all been headed by Spanish soldiers, and they were royalists. They resented the rule of Mexico, which knew and cared little about their problems. California easily might have joined another monarchy.

But what might have happened didn't happen. After three more years the Russians abandoned Rossiya, though they did not formally give it up till 1841. Then John Sutter bought the buildings, Russia ceded the land to Mexico, and it became part of Sutter's "empire." At Fort Ross today you will find a few descendants of Russian settlers and a few orchards of apples native to the far north, or at least to areas as far north as apples grow. The Russian River also is named for them. But the only vivid reminder of the Russian occupation is found in the often told but still fresh and fragrant story of Concepcion Arguello and the handsome young chamberlain of the Czar.

Yankee Henry Fitch of New Bedford, Massachusetts, had much better luck. A land where hides were so plentiful they could be gathered up by shiploads was a gold coast for New England mariners, but when Captain Fitch's ship put in at San Diego it wasn't hides that attracted him. It was Josefa Carrillo. Her name wasn't really Josefa but Maria Antonia Natalia Elijia. She had so many names that her godmother forgot what they were and called her Josefa during the baptismal ceremony, and the name stuck all her life. Legend says Josefa was such a dazzling girl that Governor Echeandia, who was a rather bad boy, wanted her himself. However that may be, the dashing Fitch captivated her and some of her relatives, and, on his promise to become a Roman Catholic and be naturalized, a marriage was hastily planned. But Governor Echeandia forbade it, saying that it was against the law for Californians to marry foreigners. Feeling that the *fait accompli* was the best answer to that, a priest was in the act of marrying the young lovers when a man strode into the small and select wedding party and shouted: "In the name of the Governor, I forbid the banns!"

Governor Echeandia was making his home in San Diego "because of the charms of its ladies" and seemed much inclined to move the capital there from Monterey. The Governor had so much power in those days that both Josefa's family and the padre, who was on her side, may have had reasons they did not voice for wishing to see Josefa out of his reach. But neither protests nor pleadings could prevail against the decree, so Josefa whispered something to Captain Fitch, and then both meekly submitted.

The next day Captain Fitch bade farewell to the Carrillos and the many friends he had made in San Diego, and toward evening both his brig, the "Maria Ester," and her companion ship, the "Vulture," set sail.

No doubt Governor Echeandia smiled with satisfaction as those white sails reddened and vanished into the sunset like rosy dreams. But late that night a horse carrying double raced along the hoof-muffling sand of the beach skirting Point Loma, now part of San Diego but then miles from the little town. And what do you think? There the riders came on a gig beached on the sand, and beside it was Captain Henry Fitch.

The two riders dismounted. The man, Don Pio Pico, later to be a Governor of California himself, kissed his Cousin Josefa good-by and wrapped a serape about her for warmth, and she was off with Captain Fitch in his gig.

They did not go to the "Maria Ester" but to the "Vulture," where Fitch placed his bride in care of his friend, Captain Barry, in order to protect her good name. The two ships sailed for South America, and in Valparaiso Captain Barry, who had been a guest at the interrupted wedding, saw the ceremony completed.

Wounding the ego of a rather vain Governor was not a thing to be done with safety, however. A year later, Captain Fitch and his wife and baby returned to California, landing at San Pedro. The word quickly got around, and Father Sanchez, head of Mission San Gabriel, felt it his duty to summon the young couple before him on "charges most serious." Captain Fitch responded to the summons, displayed his marriage certificate, and sailed away to Monterey with his family. But a whispering campaign had filled the mind of Father Sanchez with doubts, and it may be that his own ego was a bit ruffled. Or maybe it was because Governor Echeandia had returned to Monterey. Anyway, the padre sent to Monterey an order for the arrest and return of the culprit to San Gabriel. Echeandia leaped at the chance. He ordered Fitch returned to San Gabriel and Josefa detained in Monterey.

Fitch contested every step taken against him. Josefa was placed in the care of a Captain Cooper and his wife. Fitch declared that his ship was not ready to sail and that he could not make the trip by land. The Monterey authorities hotly contested his plea to be allowed to sail to San Pedro in his own brig, asserting that once he put out to sea there

was no telling where he would land, and finally he
had to put up bond big enough to soothe the feelings of the authorities in case he did fail to show up
at San Gabriel. But it all took time and gave the
Fitches a chance to line up their friends and sympathizers.

Fitch stopped to trade at Santa Barbara and other
places and took several months to get to San Pedro.
In the meantime Doña Josefa was not idle. With
the Coopers on her side, she argued it would be better for her to go to San Gabriel, where she and her
husband were to be tried for their alleged offense.
Finally she managed to be placed in the care of
Doña Eulalia Perez, who directed the women
neophytes at Mission San Gabriel, teaching them
everything from housework to the making of clothing and even altar cloths. Much of the Indian art
of today, including Navajo silversmithing, was
taught by the Spanish missionaries.

When Don Enrique arrived, he came as a
prisoner, guarded as if he were a pirate, and Josefa
was removed to the home of a Mrs. William
Richardson. Fitch's ship was impounded, too, and
things looked dark for the Fitches. But they and
their friends kept fighting, and Governor Echeandia
seems to have stood none too well with some of the
clergy. Enrique and Josefa were called before the
ecclesiastical court repeatedly, and the validity of

their Valparaiso marriage certificate was sternly questioned, but, as public sympathy changed, and Echeandia became less and less popular, it suddenly appeared that the charge was all wrong—Echeandia had caused the arrest without ecclesiastical authority, and for that infringement he himself should be considered "a culprit before God's tribunal."

How much of that change of heart was due to Spanish love of romance and the influence of California's intermarried first families it is impossible to say at this late date. But the eventual decision was that "the Fiscal has not substantiated his accusations, the marriage at Valparaiso, though not legitimate, is not null but valid; I therefore order the parties to be set at liberty and the wife given up to her husband; and that they be present next Sunday, receiving the sacraments that should have preceded the marriage ceremony. Yet, considering the great scandal which Don Enrique has caused in this province, I condemn him to give, as a penance and reparation, a bell of at least 50 pounds in weight to the church in Los Angeles, which has only a borrowed one. And further I command the couple to present themselves in church with lighted candles in their hands for three *dias festivos* and recite together for thirty days one-third of the rosary of the Holy Virgin."

And though some historians credit Echeandia with being an honest gentleman, striving only for the best, tradition generally speaks harshly of the man who tried to stand in the way of romance.

But even though they broke the rules of church and state and the laws of family life, which said it couldn't happen there, such love affairs between Californians and friendly enemies were as nothing compared to that of lovely Guadalupe Ortega and Pirate Joe. It happened in 1818, when Hippolyte Bouchard, the French pirate, carrying letters of marque from Argentina, almost conquered California. It seems fair to call Bouchard a pirate, despite the letters of marque, for neither he nor his men owed allegiance to Argentina. The 285 men are said to have been of all races, colors, and habits, and the officer in charge of the smaller of his two ships was from Massachusetts.

Though this was forty-nine years after Spain had occupied California by colonization, its capital, Monterey, was too weak to fight off the two ships and the 285 men, though the shore battery fired at the ships for some two hours before the pirates landed and sacked the town. Then they sailed south to the rich Ortega Rancho and sacked and burned it, and then south again to Santa Barbara, and then to the rich mission of San Juan Capistrano. In one of those seizures one officer and two black men started to come ashore in a small boat, which capsized in the high surf. The two black men tried to swim back to their ship but could not make it. One was drowned, and vaqueros rescued the other with lassos. But the legend declares that when the white man, who was an officer, was lassoed, he trod water and dragged the vaquero and his horse out into the surf. A second vaquero came to the aid of the first, and the mighty pirate dragged him and his horse into the water, too. But the third one lassoed him so that his arms were bound to his sides, and he was dragged ashore, helpless, and made a prisoner.

By that time the Spaniards seem to have been divided between admiration for their prisoner's prowess and a desire for vengeance for the misdeeds of the pirates. Governor Sola had sent the women and children of Monterey to the interior mission of Soledad before the pirates landed, but in some other places the surprise was complete, and "they forced the women to dance with them." At any rate, there were plenty of Californians who wished to deal violently with their captive, Pirate Joe, and he would have been put to death had not Guadalupe Ortega, whose home had been robbed and burned by the pirates, pleaded for his life.

Pirate Joe was a builder and a hard worker. Down in Los Angeles the Plaza Church had progressed very slowly. Even though the padres at San Gabriel Mission, already famous for its good wines and brandies, had promised the residents of Los Angeles seven barrels of brandy as compensation for building the church, the work had stopped as soon as the workers ran out of brandy. The *mañana* habit was distressing the good padres. So Joseph Chapman went into the San Gabriel Mountains, felled great trees, and hauled them down to Los Angeles, twenty miles away. They still tell you in that church that it wouldn't have had a roof but for José Juan Chapman, which was the name under which Pirate Joe was baptized when he had worked out his penance, and in 1832, in the charming chapel at Santa Ynez, he married Guadalupe Ortega, the little girl who had saved his life fourteen years before.

Californians still ride forth in quest of romance, but not on horses now. They are more addicted to motor cars than any other people. Not counting public conveyances, Los Angeles County averages one motor vehicle to every two and one-half persons, which may explain why so many of its drivers seem to feel it their obligation to halve a few persons daily. With beach, mountain, and desert resorts, and Old Mexico all within 150 miles, the Angeleno thinks nothing of driving several hundred miles just to see what he can see. The infinite variety of climate, scenery, and activity within easy reach has got Californians into the gadding habit, and wherever they go they are seeking something about which to get excited. And wasn't that what inspired Cabrillo and Sir Francis Drake, Coronado and Rezanov, Jedediah Smith and Frémont, Richard Henry Dana and all the rest?

No CALIFORNIA custom is older than that of gambling. The soldiers who accompanied the Portolá and De Anza expeditions could find little else to amuse them. The Indians they met loved gambling at first sight, and even the pretty beads and the stories of heaven by which they were attracted could not get the grip on them that gambling did.

When California became a political unit, every

youth was subject to military service when he reached the age of sixteen, and it is recognized that young men in military establishments go into gambling with a certain fervor. In that sweet pastoral era, the children bet the buttons off their clothes on all sorts of childish games and were encouraged to do so by their elders, who often backed them with money. "Often," writes Nellie von der Grift Sanchez, "urchins might be seen without a button on their clothes, all having been cut off by them and laid on the altar of fortune." De Anza wrote of the colonists he took to found Yerba Buena that they were so poor the government would have to feed and clothe them, for "whatever money they got they gambled away."

The rodeo was a California invention. There is even a town in California named Rodeo, which had its beginnings as a place where the horsemen of various ranchos met to compete in races and vaquero contests of all kinds—and there was gambling aplenty on all the contests.

The sporting spirit of Spanish California is indicated by the historic race between Sarco and Black Swan, though it occurred in 1852, more than five years after the surrender of the Californians to United States forces. Don Pio Pico, last Mexican governor, owned vast estates, but his pride was Sarco, a gray stallion which triumphed at every rodeo or other event at which there was racing. Don José Sepulveda was proud of his grand estates, too, and of his magnificent horses. He matched horse after horse against Sarco, and Sarco always won with ease.

In the way which has become their custom, Californians boasted that Sarco was the greatest horse in the world. But a sailor who had seen more of the world than had most of the boasters said that in Australia there was a horse named Black Swan which could beat Sarco. Don José looked up the sailor and was so impressed he secretly sent an agent to Australia to buy Black Swan.

Don José went to San Francisco to meet the horse, but there was no fanfare about it. He took the horse to his ranch and kept it there for weeks before he issued a challenge to Don Pio.

The racers were to start at the Plaza in Los Angeles, proceed to a point four and one-half miles south on San Pedro Road, and return to the starting point. Horses were horses in those days, and three leagues—nine miles—was the derby route.

Besides twenty-five thousand dollars in gold, each of the rancheros put up five hundred horses, five hundred mares, five hundred cows, five hundred calves, and five hundred sheep. Private coinage had been permitted in California since the Gold Rush, the Wells Fargo Company and others having made gold slugs valued at fifty dollars, and before the race Señora Sepulveda went about her ranch with her apron full of those slugs, giving them to her servants to bet on the contest.

None but the most essential work was done by anybody in all southern California the day of the race.

They were off on scheduled time, with Sarco in the lead. It was Sarco at the sixteenth by ten lengths, Sarco at the eighth by fifteen lengths, Sarco at the quarter by seventeen lengths, Sarco at the half—the turning point, four and one-half miles from the start—by twelve lengths, Sarco at the three-quarters by six lengths, and Sarco into the stretch—the last half-league—by a head. Then for a mile the two gallant horses ran neck and neck, and those who were watching had their hearts in their necks. But half a mile from the finish line Black Swan went ahead and came home an easy winner. There is no way of estimating the number of horses, saddles, bridles, and serapes that were wagered by relatives, friends, and adherents of the two princely rancheros. Every vaquero and nearly every citizen wagered something. Indians bet their blankets and Chinese laundrymen bet their secret savings. The race more or less affected the prosperity of every family.

To Gamble on Anything

Young caballeros setting forth on tours of inspection—of the crop of señoritas—laid wagers as to how many hearts they could break and what tokens of affection they could bring home. And the young men weren't the only ones. Every youth who rode forth wore his lady's colors in the form of some personal adornment beautifully embroidered by her. Whenever he whispered burning words to another señorita the latter, pretending ignorance of the significance of those tokens, suggested that the gallant youth give them to her as keepsakes, and quite frequently the faithless rascal did that very thing. The girls of Santa Barbara so consistently got away with love tokens into which the Los Angeles girls had stitched their hearts that the latter made up a song which ran:

"Las Barbaranas son bonitas y poquitas,
  Pero perigunas como las animas banditas."

Roughly translated, this means the Santa Barbara girls were pretty and little, but bandits.

The girls, too, were doing a little wagering on the number of conquests they could boast.

But early Californians gambled for excitement, not for avarice. The Gold Rush brought an orgy of gambling—for money, for gold dust, for nuggets, for claims, for the favors of the first career women

California ever saw, the prostitutes. The miners would bet on anything, from how far a frog would jump—the inspiration of the story that made Mark Twain famous—to how many Chinese would be murdered next week.

When Marshall picked up the nugget which made news around the world, there wasn't a laundry in San Francisco, and men poured in so fast in the months after Sam Brannan exhibited a bottle of gold dust that shiploads of laundry were sent all the way to China, if the Chinese laundries in Hawaii already were overloaded. Wealthy Chinese came in who saw the chance to send home for hundreds of other Chinese, holding them in virtual slavery till they worked out their passage money and no one knows how much more. It was a sixteen-hour work day for those hapless men and women, but somehow a group of them got to every major mining camp. They had a method of their own of "sweating" gold coins, when coins began to take the place of dust. In those days the coins did not have milled edges, so the Chinese would file a little off the edge of each coin and contrive to exchange the bits for a new coin. There was even private coinage, as has already been pointed out, till a branch of the United States Mint was established in San Francisco in 1854. It was to stop the sweating practice, it is believed in California, that the milled-edge coin was invented. Even then the Chinese would fill a buckskin bag with gold coins and shake them vigorously with Chinese patience until there was a little gold dust in the bag. In the camps the Chinese washed out gold, too, and got a little to boot from the clothing they washed. One way and another they would amass considerable quantities of gold, more or less as a community project, and, when some gambler who had gone broke at the gaming table needed dust to go back and gamble again, often the simplest and quickest way to get it was to murder a few Chinese. The law of 1850 held that a white man could not be convicted on the testimony of an Indian, and a later court ruling held that a Chinese was an Indian, so far as the intent of the law went.

But it took San Francisco and the reign of Ralston the Magnificent to bring gambling to its most grandiose excesses. San Francisco organized its Stock and Exchange Board in 1862 to lift gambling to a more pretentious level, so it would interest the outside world, and soon it became the town's madhouse for both men and women. George Lyman, in *Ralston's Ring*,* tells of the long line of carriages drawing up to it one day in 1864 to disgorge "the ladies" of San Francisco, women who might not

* Quotations from this book by permission of Charles Scribner's Sons.

meet at any other place but found the lure of gambling the great leveler. There were, he says, "ladies in fine carriages with downy fur-cushioned interiors, beautiful ladies, ladies in rustling silks, mysterious women in flowing black veils, perfumed women with sparkling eyes, flashing teeth and diamond-studded ears. The ladies were hurrying to the eleven o'clock session of the Stock and Exchange Board to gamble on Comstock shares. Some were the wives of operators, others of plungers, but the vast majority were victims of the Comstock. The prodigious wealth of the lode and the excitement had weaned them from their homes, their school rooms, and the city's bright lights. Silk-hatted curb brokers milled excitedly about the entrance. San Francisco had become a gambling city the like of which had never been known on the Coast."

As the city had been given only sixty-four thousand residents by the recent census, that was putting it mildly. It is doubtful if any other community was ever seized by such a gambling fever. Bartenders, ditch diggers, and peddlers were becoming plutocrats, beggars of yesterday were riding in showy carriages, behind magnificent horses, to gingerbread castles they were building. Every penny a great many of those people could lay their hands on went into Comstock shares. Church treasurers "invested" church funds. Ministers "invested" their salaries. Housewives "invested" the cash with which they had set out to pay the grocer. For Mr. Ralston was a wonderful man and Mr. Ralston knew and Mr. Ralston always said, "Buy Comstock."

William Chapman Ralston had been some sort of clerk on an Ohio River steamboat. When he heard of the Gold Rush he borrowed three hundred dollars to get to California. That took him down to Panama and across the Isthmus, but that was all. Thousands of Americans were stranded there. Many were dying of tropical maladies. Many had gone broke because when a ship arrived from San Francisco it could usually carry only one-fourth of those seeking transportation. Some had waited there so long and grown so desperate they made log canoes and set sail in them for San Francisco, which none of them ever reached.

When the steamer "New Orleans" limped into Panama in 1851, Ralston was waiting. Illness had knocked its captain off the bridge. Ralston might not have been able to get on the ship but for his steamboat experience. He had never been on a seagoing ship before he sailed to Panama. He had never been more than a clerk on a river boat. But he was a confident gambler. He sailed the "New Orleans" back to San Francisco, a trip that has tricked many a seasoned sea captain into a wreck off Point Arguello or some other deceptive place along the coast.

San Francisco then was such a mudhole that a horse might drown in the mud on Montgomery Street, its best street. But the magnificent land-locked harbor protected by the Golden Gate thrilled the river-boat clerk. So did the swaggering, lawless, determined, hell-can't-stop-us spirit of the town. He determined to stay there and grow with it into greatness. And in ten years he had become its leader. "Nothing in California," says Lyman, "could be accomplished socially, politically or financially without the backing of Ralston."

It was Ralston who inspired the Stock and Exchange Board. It was Ralston who organized the Bank of California. It was Ralston who lent Leland Stanford money to drag his railroad over the last range of mountains, linking California to the rest of the country by bands of steel. It was Ralston who built the "Yankee Blade" and was so eager for it to beat the thirty-four other ships which were taking off for Panama at the same time that its captain took too many risks, and it went down off Point Arguello with three hundred passengers and $153,000 in gold. But Ralston was undaunted.

At the age of thirty-eight, Ralston had something to say about every worthwhile industry in California, every ship sailing to Alaska or the Orient, every boat on the inland waters—and some noted steamboats were plying the Sacramento and San Joaquin rivers and San Francisco Bay then. It was Ralston who built theaters which were dazzlingly magnificent and gave diamond necklaces to actresses he admired. As a crowning glory, it was Ralston who built the Palace Hotel, making it more luxurious than anything in New York at that time, though San Francisco could barely chin the 250,000 mark in population.

Ralston had absolute faith in the future of his city and was determined it should have the best. He wanted the Palace to be its show window, its inspiration. He bought a ranch covered with oak forest to have the oak specially milled into lumber for the Palace. He started a foundry for the making of nails and tools for it. He built a colossal furniture factory, sure that the furniture of California laurel which would be its first product would arouse so much admiration in the Palace that all the country would want it. He started a lock and key factory, as all the locks and keys in the Palace must be striking and individual, and not only every room but every closet and dresser drawer was to have its key. That was only a few years after Black Bart, in the Mother Lode country, had aroused suspicion at Grandma Rollerie's little inn because he had asked for a key for his room, a thing no one had ever asked for before.

The elevators for the Palace had to be specially designed. There had to be an interior court of "splendid proportions and matchless beauty." That marble-pillared court was 144 feet long by 84 feet wide. "On the ground floor," says *Ralston's Ring,* was "a circular driveway wide enough for a coach and four to turn, paved with marble. Light standards with multicolored globes made it a scene of pagan splendor."

On the top floor was a crystal roof garden, mostly art bronze and glass, with hundreds of hanging baskets of flowers and deep red carpets. Against the colonnades, orange, lime, and lemon trees in particolored Italian vases were banked. The ballroom was magnificent, and the dining room could seat twelve hundred guests. All the china was eggshell Haviland, the glassware was cut crystal, and the linen was Irish linen, everything being specially designed for the Palace.

In the huge kitchens a special chef presided over each department, from soups to ices, and all were encouraged to let their imaginations go the limit in preparing dishes which would make the guests exclaim. Every guest room had a rug specially made in Glasgow and a great bay window, so that the guests might look out in more than one direction.

There were also "committee rooms," in which groups could play poker, or one might "entertain a lady without fear of intrusion." In every room ticked a handsome clock made especially for the Palace in Ralston's Cornell Watch Factory in Oakland, and from Ralston's Mission Woolen Mills came the thousands of pairs of blankets. The drapes were all of silk, spun from California cocoons in a factory started by Ralston to promote the industry in California. The basement alone, with its swimming pool, was said to have cost $1,700,000, and Ralston seemed ready to spend a million more on each of the seven floors. The wines were from the Ralston Vineyards. Even the tobacco was from the Ralston fields at Gilroy.

All that was a prodigious and fantastic gamble, an advertising campaign to impress all America and part of Europe with the wealth, the possibilities, and the great future of California. It made the art dealers in Italy, the millers in Glasgow, the bankers in London all conscious of the fact that the Comstock Lode was said to be producing thirty-six million dollars' worth of silver a year, and Ralston was said to be the great man of the Comstock. And it was so successful that for several years New York and London bankers were ready to finance any new project of Ralston's, the young wizard of the West.

Ralston's theater drew the greatest of the stage

to California, and every one of them went away
as a press agent after a magnificent entertainment
at Ralston's country place, Belmont. No one could
ever forget a visit to Belmont, for Ralston drove his
guests there himself, behind relays of horses so fast
they always beat the train. There were weekly
banquets at Belmont which returned travelers told
about with awe in London and Paris and Berlin.
Those reports caused Bismarck to demonetize silver
in Germany, after even the director of the United
States Mint estimated that billions would come
from the Comstock.

There was such faith in Ralston that the United
States Treasury would let him borrow a few hundred thousand if he should be temporarily short of
loose change, half a century before the Reconstruc-
tion Finance Corporation was thought of.

Unquestionably Ralston's visions woke California
to the realization that it had far more than its own
gold and Nevada's silver to draw on and build with.
But his successes inspired competition, and his bril-
liance aroused envy. No man could back so many
enterprises and squander so lavishly without being
caught short some time.

In the end it was four Irishmen of humble beginnings who were his undoing. They were John William Mackay, James C. Flood, James Graham Fair,
and William S. O'Brien.

To Gamble on Anything

Fair was only eighteen years old when he arrived in California, but he was the leader of the party he brought overland from St. Louis. Before that he had been an Irish immigrant. In Carson Hills he met and married Teresa Rooney, who ran a boarding house, and the boarding house of a girl young enough to attract an eighteen-year-old boy couldn't have been much of an institution. Fair barely made wages for some years as a miner, but one day he trailed a group of Chileans who always seemed to find enough gold for a good time and discovered where they got it. Mackay was another Irish immigrant, who worked as a mucker in the Virginia City mines at $4.50 a day. He married Louise Bryant, a young widow who was supporting her baby daughter by sewing for Comstock miners. Flood and O'Brien were saloon keepers. They sold good liquor to miners and listened attentively to what those they trusted said.

When they landed in California all four of those Irishmen were what we would call mere boys today. The eldest was twenty-three, and when they met in the saloon of Flood and O'Brien the saloon keepers were the only ones who had any community standing in San Francisco, though Mackay had worked up to shift boss and then to superintendent in the mines.

Later, when immense wealth had unlocked the

golden gate of society, Fair became a United States Senator, and the Fair mansion on Nob Hill was a social center of San Francisco. His daughter Teresa married Herman Oelrichs, and his daughter Virginia, named for Virginia City, where she was born, became Mrs. William K. Vanderbilt, Jr. When New York society, forgetting its own humble beginnings, sniffed a little at Mrs. Mackay, she tilted her own nose higher, and the Mackays went to London. When the official Gazette reported, in 1889, that the Prince of Wales had honored Mrs. Mackay by being her guest for dinner, the Mackays were "in." Mrs. Mackay was received by Queen Victoria, their London home was a place sought by "the best people." In Paris, too, Mrs. Mackay presided over a brilliant salon. Her daughter, Eva Bryant, became the Princess Colonna, her sister was married to a count. She bought the Shah of Persia's pearls, the Czar of Russia's tapestries, and tried to buy the Arc de Triomphe! Possibly she wanted to give that to Mackay for a watch charm. As a financial power in New York, Mackay quarreled with Jay Gould and, mainly to annoy his enemy, who was the main power in Western Union, joined forces with James Gordon Bennett in launching the Postal Telegraph as a competing service.

But that is getting ahead of our story. The four Irishmen began in a very small way, but they were aggressive. They could see the cracks in Ralston's defenses when no one else could. They encouraged Lucky Baldwin to sell out to Ralston for $3,600,000. They began to battle Ralston for control of the Comstock. They made the Ralston interests spend $800,000 to win a senatorial election in Nevada. They still kept both their money and their bullion in Ralston's bank and apparently recognized his leadership as the rest of San Francisco and Virginia City did, but they were in the game for keeps.

Rumors started that Ralston had overextended himself. A New York financial editor mentioned them. When Ralston needed ready money, New York suddenly grew hesitant. So did the Oriental Bank of London, which never before had hesitated. So did the United States Treasury, which previously had seemed to take pleasure in backing the great constructive genius of the West. And then "The Irish" started the Nevada Bank of California, challenging the leadership of Ralston's California Bank, and called on Ralston to turn over their deposit of $1,800,000 as well as their bullion.

When one George Upshur handed Ralston a note from Flood withdrawing those assets, Ralston only smiled confidently.

"Go back and tell Flood I'll send him back to selling rum over the Auction Lunch Counter," he said.

Upshur delivered the message and came back with the reply: "Mr. Flood says in short time he will be able to sell rum over the counter of the Bank of California."

On August 26, 1875, after the whole country had been shaken by the panic of 1873, the crash came, and Ralston, still smiling, still apparently confident, surrendered all his properties—his villa at Belmont, his town house on Pine Street, the still-unfinished Palace, and his many enterprises—and still owed over four million dollars. He was asked to resign the presidency of the Bank of California. And then, as was his habit when he wished to relax, the most dazzling gambler of them all went out for a swim in the ocean—and never came back.

Whether, pondering his problems, he swam out too far unintentionally or by intent is anybody's guess. Just before that swim he seemed as debonair and confident as ever, asserting he would start life again without a dollar and soon be on top of the heap. But the sea he had laughed at many a time was as ruthless as Flood, Fair, Mackay, and O'Brien when its chance came, and Ralston the Magnificent was drowned.

California's readiness to gamble on anything infected William H. Brown, a New Yorker, to gamble on building a sumptuous steamboat to ply the Sacramento River. It was called the "New World," for

California was a new world then. Like Ralston, Brown wanted nothing but the costliest, and his visions outran his purse. The handsomely furnished boat, with gaming tables and everything, was ready to launch, when some creditors who hadn't been paid got nervous and libeled the craft. Deputy sheriffs came aboard and tacked on the pilothouse door a notice that the boat must be sold at public auction, on the courthouse steps, to satisfy judgments.

But steam was up, everything was ready for a festive launching, and Brown and Captain Ned Wakefield convinced the deputies it would be best for all concerned if the boat was launched. It would bring a better price on the auction block and help everyone. And wouldn't the deputies like some of the liquid refreshments provided for the occasion?

After all, with a crowd gathered, why spoil a party? So the "New World" was launched—and set right out to leave the old world. The deputies were entertained with enthusiasm but suddenly realized they were getting far from shore. They ordered Captain Wakefield to return at once, but he retorted he was the law on the high seas. It ended with the deputies being put over the side in a rowboat, and the "New World" steamed on. It steamed around the Horn, which in itself was a terrific gamble for a steamboat, and when it steamed into the Golden Gate in August, 1850, three months after its launching, it had picked up enough passengers on the way to make its maiden voyage extremely profitable. It is said it made one million dollars in its first year on the Sacramento, and Brown was able to pay off in full. He had won a gamble and a race against any orders which would have caused interception of the boat en route, for there was no telegraph then, and this was a full year before the "Flying Cloud" broke all records of sailing ships by sailing from New York to San Francisco in eighty-one days and twenty-one hours.

Professional gamblers still say Californians are "the gamblingest people on earth" and reap handsome annual profits from them. In 1947, the state legalized 262 days of horse-racing with pari-mutuel betting, and the total wagered at Santa Anita racetrack, on what used to be Lucky Baldwin's ranch near Los Angeles, during the midwinter meeting of fifty-five days, was $123,436,952. Gambling ships, anchored outside the three-mile limit, for years have been a problem to the authorities, for they are beyond the range of either taxes or rakeoff, but in 1946 the authorities got the Coast Guard to impound "Admiral" Tony Cornero's floating gambling palace after it had operated only three days, on the ground it had been licensed for coastwise trading but was not even equipped with motive power. In those three days, however, its profits appear to have been $173,000, according to court testimony. At Calneva, on the border between California and Nevada, there is a club house which is partly in California, partly in Nevada, and it is said that when California authorities descend on it they never find anything illegal on the California side but much activity on the Nevada side—and vice versa.

Around Lake Tahoe there are slot machines even in groceries and drugstores, the patriotic citizens arguing they make it a little less necessary for visitors to go across the line to Reno to get divorced from their small change, for the average well-patronized slot machine is said to pay a profit in excess of one hundred dollars a day. Around Palm Springs, too, anyone with a hundred dollars or more in his pocket can usually find a "club" which will accept him as a member as long as his money lasts. But, despite all those efforts, there is a continual stream of northern Californians going to Reno and of southern Californians going to Las Vegas, where gambling is the main industry, and to Tia Juana and Agua Caliente, Mexico, where there are all kinds of gambling both indoors and at the Caliente racetrack.

In the San Diego Club they show you the Billion Dollar Room, papered with the beautiful gold-sealed stock certificates of oil and mining companies which never got any further than the stock-selling stage but tempted tens of thousands of Californians to part with their savings in the hope of striking it rich. Even the city of Long Beach gambles in oil, for its wells in its harbor alone yield it about one million dollars a month in revenue, besides the taxes it collects from Signal Hill, where there is a forest of derricks. Bookmaking on football, baseball, and all the major professional and amateur sports flourishes in Los Angeles and San Francisco, and sometimes one even hears bookie odds quoted on oratorical and debating contests. Nearly everyone in California seems to feel that somehow or other Lady Luck is going to make him rich, and most of those who haven't yet bought gold bricks are saving up their money to be ready when the opportunity comes. Thrift and caution may be all right for some people, but Californians are too impulsive and too much in a hurry to put much stock in anything but taking chances.

BANCROFT says that in California's pastoral days anyone could travel from San Diego to Sonoma without a cent of money, and live handsomely all the way. Indeed, he might even find himself in a chamber in which, for his convenience, there was a bowl of coins by his bed, that being a custom with the best families. He was given the key to the gate of the rancho and assured "the house is yours." All members of the household were supposed to be his servants. If his horse had gone lame or met with any misfortune he could just leave it there and take another one. A ranchero of those days might say "Have a horse" as casually as today one might say "Have a cigarette."

Father Crespi, who logged the Portolá expedition in 1769, wrote thus of Indian hospitality:

"We saw a very pleasant and spacious valley. We stopped close to a very large pool. Near it we found a large village of heathen, very friendly and docile. They offered us their seeds in baskets. We counted more than 200 men, women and children. Each of them brought us some food. The next day was Sunday and we rested, receiving numerous visits from heathen, who came to see us from distant parts."

Driving north from Los Angeles over Sepulveda Boulevard today, one follows almost the exact route of the Indian trail Portolá followed into the San Fernando Valley, and the present town of Encino marks the spot where Portolá met those friendly Indians.

Those first Spanish invaders made a sincere effort to mollify the Indians. As late as 1798, Governor Borica, in making a land grant, bound the grantee "not to prejudice the neighboring missions and to treat both Christian and gentile Indians with that love and charity so much recommended by the laws; but not for this, to forbear carrying out the proper precautions."

Every visitor to California in its pastoral days wrote of its hospitality. South America was also a pastoral area, yet it was José Arnaz, who sailed to California from Peru, who wrote:

"They [the Californians] were great people to go visiting their friends and relatives, the whole family going and staying a week or a month. Sometimes fifty would alight on a place together, when the tortilla makers would get no rest, day or night. Of a bullock slaughtered one day there would not be enough left for breakfast next morning." And another early visitor wrote: "There is no working class among the Spaniards. The Indians do all the hard work. A rich man looks and dresses like a grandee, whilst even a miserably poor individual has the appearance of a broken down gentleman. It is not uncommon to see a man of fine figure, dressed in broadcloth and velvet and mounted on a noble horse covered with trappings, who perhaps has not a *real* in his pocket."

It's a present-day California custom to call even a half-acre flower-bulb garden a ranch, but in those days the ranches were those estates on which livestock raising was the chief occupation, the agricultural estates being known as *haciendas*. On both, at first, the dwellings were adobe huts. But mud and workers are all one needs to make adobe bricks, and those landed gentry had plenty of both. Room after room was added till the houses resembled fortresses, with walls six or seven feet thick for protection against both weather and possible enemies. A typical house would have four rooms across the front, two more behind each of the corner rooms, and a row of four across the back, making a square. All the rooms would face on a square patio, with a fountain, grass, flowers, and big trees to cool it. Behind the house, but often attached to it, might be servants' quarters and stables, flanking another patio. The world was shut out, and all the beauty and privacy were within.

When guests arrived in numbers, only the women slept indoors. The Californian was used to using his saddle for a pillow, his serape for a blanket, and the earth for a bed. No house was big enough to provide sleeping quarters for a huge family and a horde of guests.

Family life was full of ceremony and dignity, of deference to all one's elders and an almost reverential attitude toward parents. Pio Pico wrote that up to the age of twenty-six he was "under the rigid command of my lady mother, my father being dead, who never permitted me to go out of the house after eight o'clock at night." Yet on occasions Don Pio told his friends of some quite lively adventures in his youth. Walter Colton, alcalde of Monterey in 1846, wrote that "usage here allows a mother to chastise her son till he is married and lives in his own house," and it was the privilege of any elderly person to correct or even whip any young person. Even a man of fifty dared not sit or smoke or wear his hat in the presence of his father unless commanded to do so, and it was not unusual for fathers to chastise grown sons with the lash. Yet they were effusively affectionate, and nothing delighted a ranchero more than to have his fifteen children and their wives and husbands and children drop in on him for a week or a month.

It was a common thing for families to ride horseback thirty miles to go to church and three times that far to attend a *baile*. On the way home from church, a whole cavalcade of several families might stop at the first rancho. There the men killed a bullock while the women set about household tasks as if at home. If the host rancher had no suitable bullock, it was quite all right to borrow one from a neighbor.

In all pioneering societies, people learn to rely on one another. From birth to death, it is the right of persons in the wilderness to call on anyone within reach for help, and the unwritten law compels the giving of that help. That was the unwritten law of California, and whether the event was a christening, a marriage, or a funeral, everyone within reach was expected to attend without invitation, and word was sent to all relatives whose homes were distant. It is pretty hard not to have a comradely feeling for anyone who has helped you in time of trouble, danger, or rejoicing. Not only were the Californians bound by such ties and by intermarriage of families, but anyone who stood as godfather or godmother was a *compadre* or *comadre,* a position equaling that of blood relative among those people. And such loyalties grew out of the assistance neighbors who lived from thirty to one hundred miles apart continually had to give one another, under such conditions, that friendship became as high a duty as honor. If the man you called *"me valedor"* was in danger, and to help him meant risking your life, you were supposed to risk it for him, as he would for you.

With such bonds of blood, religion, and friendship, with so many Indians to do the work that one who had reason to go could always be spared, and with such abundance that no one who visited a day or a month felt he was doing other than a kindness to his hosts, it was natural that Californians should become habitual visitors. There wasn't much else to do, except when a ship came to port.

When Californians grew rich, according to Bancroft, it was not because of thrift but because they could not spend the accumulation. "Life then was unlike any of the modifications of feudal Europe," he says. "It was unlike the fixed features of Oriental society, the nomadic communities of Arabia or the aristocratic tribes of America or any of the great types of society, aboriginal or colonial, that ever existed before. Luxury and pleasure there were an abundance of, but they were of such a character as not to be dependent on money or wealth."

Seventy-five years after Monterey was established, Walter Colton wrote that that capital's hospitality was such that "a public hotel had never been able to exist." Colton, by the way, was one of the *gringos* California girls were not even supposed to meet. Like William Heath Davis, Abel Stearns, Alfred Robinson, Benjamin Wilson, and many others who have given pictures of Spanish California life as seen through Yankee eyes, Colton married one of the flashing-eyed señoritas and became an important figure in Monterey. Besides being alcalde of Monterey he was the builder of Colton Hall, in which California's Constitutional Convention was held in 1849.

Land grants were made only in rare cases at first, and in more than fifty years fewer than fifty grants had been made. In the 1840's, however, the Mexican governors either feared United States occupation or began passing out grants as political favors, or both, for in all 1,045 were made. Portolá's 200 head of cattle, and a few more brought by De Anza, had produced such large California families that in the early 1840's there were 1,200,000 cattle in California.

But even the princely land grants of Spanish days did not compare with the vast cattle empire of Henry Miller, a San Francisco butcher who, with a partner named Lux, decided to raise his own cattle. By 1858 he was powerful enough to have his name changed, by special act of the Legislature, from Henri or Heinrich Kreiser. His lands extended from near Bakersfield, in Southern California, almost to San Francisco Bay on the west, over into Nevada on the east, and up into Oregon on the north. The easterly and westerly tips of his domain were more than five hundred miles apart, as were the northerly and southerly tips.

The Gold Rush had brought many tramps to California, and Miller gave orders that they should always be given a night's lodging and a meal. That was hospitality with a purpose—to prevent damage and theft. But he always let his employees eat first and then fed the itinerants out of the same plates, as the hungry tramps would lick the platters so clean they would need little washing. Nevertheless, one could travel hundreds of miles in California and be sure of food and lodging all the way if one crossed Miller's lands, and it was hard to travel far without crossing them.

Now that California leads the world in the production of agricultural wealth, the areas Miller and Lux controlled then produce more wealth than was fought for in many wars between kingdoms. It is hard to see how any one man or pair of men could get hold of so much land. The simple fact is that the carpetbaggers in the South after the War Between the States were gentlemen compared to many of the Americans who swept into California following the War with Mexico, and what they did to the hospitable, unsuspecting, and sadly unbusinesslike ranchers was something to blush about. Many persons from whom Miller and Lux acquired lands had practically stolen them.

One thing Miller did was establish stores. For more than fifty years after Portolá and De Anza brought settlers to California, the visiting ship was the only commercial institution many of the ranchers saw, and it might be six months or a year before another ship came in. In every home the women learned to sew and not only did exquisite embroidery but all the tailoring for themselves, their families, and their servants. They trained many of the Indian girls to do this, too. But of cloth and manufactured items they had none, and when a ship came in they had to buy for a period of months. New England ships brought necessities—cloth, sugar, rum, and articles made of wood and steel and tin. Ships from the Orient brought luxuries—silks, tea, ornaments. When a bonfire on a certain point informed the ranchers for fifty miles or more around that a ship was coming to port, a pack train was loaded with hides and tallow and anything else the ranch provided which the ship's company might want, and the ranchero and his wife, often riding a horse which carried double, would head the procession. Vaqueros kept the pack train in line, and the ranchero's fifty dogs brought up the rear. The ranchers had no money of their own. Hides had a money value and were accepted as money—that is the explanation of the title of Ana Begue de Packman's "Leather Dollars." Brandy also was an established medium of exchange, and a barrel containing one hundred and fifty pints was the equivalent of fifty pesos of Spanish money.

It was the missions which made the wine and brandy. With cattle on ten thousand hills, there was almost no milk, for most of the cattle were so wild it took three men to milk a cow. Two would lasso her fore and aft while the milker would take his bucket in one hand and his life in the other and get what milk he could from the frantic animal. The ranches raised fruits and vegetables for their own use only. With not a market or a village store in the land, it was a waste of energy to raise more, and the caballeros were thrifty with energy except where dancing was concerned.

Mission hospitality was as open as rancho hospitality. Jedediah Strong Smith, the first United States citizen to arrive in California overland, brought his weary party over the Cajon Pass in 1827, and a few days later they camped beside the lovely little lake which later was the centerpiece of Lucky Baldwin's Rancho Santa Anita and now is a state park and arboretum. Harrison G. Rogers, Smith's Boswell and keeper of the records of that expedition, writes of that invasion:

"[Monday, November] 27th . . . We passed innumerable herds of cattle, horses and some hundreds of sheep; we passed four or five Ind. lodges, that their Inds. acts as herdsmen. There came an old Ind. to us that speaks good Spanish and took us with him to his mansion [mission]. So soon as we enc. there was plenty prepared to eat, a fine young cow killed, and a plenty of corn meal given us; pretty soon after the 2 commandants of the missionary establishment come to us and had the appearance of gentlemen. Mr. S. went with them to the mansion and I stay with the company, there was great feasting among the men as they were pretty hungry not having any good meat for some time.

"28th: . . . About 10 o'clock at night supper was served and Mr. S. and myself sent for. I was introduced to the 2 priests over a glass of good old whiskey and found them to be very jovial friendly gentlemen, the supper consisted of a number of different dishes, served different from any table I was ever at. Plenty of good wine during supper, before the cloth was removed sigars was introduced. Mr. S. has wrote to the Governor, and I expect we shall be here some days.

"Friday, January 19th: . . . Mr. S. and myself returned to the mission, late last evening and took supper with old Father Sancus, for the last time and our farewell. The old father give each of us a blanket and give me a cheese and a gourd filled with ogadent [*aguardiente*]. All hands being ready early in the morning, we started and travelled, and had an Ind. guide."

That is enough to show that a party of alien enemies found a pretty hospitable welcome for a little visit lasting from November 27 to January 19, a longer period than most of us today would enjoy having our dearest friends visit us. Eighteenth-century Englishmen may have seen cynical truth in comparing guests to fish after the third day, but nineteenth-century Californians apparently didn't begin to notice any unpleasant aroma till after three months. In a chapter headed "Settling Book

Accounts at Santa Anita," William Heath Davis reports:

"James McKinla and myself left San Diego and went overland to Santa Anita, a few miles north of Mission San Gabriel. Hugo Reid, a Scotchman, lived at Santa Anita. He was a skilful accountant and we brought on a pack animal a large pile of account books belonging to the business of Paty, McKinla and Fitch, who were dissolving partnership. We remained at Santa Anita most of November and December, adjusting the books with his aid."

Reid's adobe still stands, within two hundred yards of the present Santa Anita Racetrack, where "book accounts" running as high as three million dollars a day are settled by totalizator in five minutes.

Another sample of California hospitality is part of the record of Helen Hunt Jackson's visit to southern California to gather material for her novel *Ramona.* From Kinneyloa, the home of Abbott Kinney, on what had been part of Rancho Santa Anita, she drove with Kinney to Riverside, then to San Jacinto, where an incident happened which gave her the climax for her story, and then to Rancho Guajome, the home of Señora Cave Couts, widow of a United States army officer who had come into possession of that vast estate by marrying

her. The Coutses had never seen or heard of Helen
Hunt Jackson before, but theirs was, and still is,
one of the most truly typical ranch homes of the
Spanish period. In 1883, the year of Mrs. Jackson's
visit, it looked and operated just as it had before the
United States owned California, and Kinney had
no hesitancy in taking Mrs. Jackson there, sure she
would be invited to remain several weeks. There
she industriously put together the notes she had
taken on visits to the Camulos Rancho, the home of
the Del Valles, San Jacinto, and several other
places.

Señora Couts was mistress of the rancho, and her
young son, Cave Couts, Jr., was a youth of about
twenty years. I have visited Rancho Guajome often
and knew that second Cave Couts well, but I never
asked him about Mrs. Jackson's visit there but once.
He believed she had used his mother as the model
for the rather unpleasant character of the Señora
in *Ramona* and himself as a model for Felipe, and
had failed to do justice in both cases. Not long before his death in 1943, he mentioned it to me and
growled: "It was no way to repay hospitality."

With a background of Spanish grandeur and
hauteur, the Gold Rush of the late forties and all
the fifties and sixties, and the land rush which has
been going on ever since, have made Californians as
a class swaggering, cocksure, self-reliant, daring,

and adventurous. They like to do things never done before or more gaudily than they were ever done before.

When San Francisco wallowed in the wealth of the Mother Lode and the Comstock Lode, its ways and its extravagances were fabulous. When the people realized that the vast resources of the land could produce more agricultural wealth, year after year, than all the mineral wealth, a different kind of affluence was born, but it tended back to the old Spanish pattern with modern improvements. In recent years Mr. William Randolph Hearst, for instance, has dispensed a fabulous hospitality at his Rancho San Simeon and at times has rivaled the whimsical prodigality of the Caliph of Baghdad.

There still are vast ranches in California. The Santa Margarita Ranch, much of which was taken for Camp Pendleton, Marine Corps training base, during the war, had more than 226,000 acres before the government commandeered that part of it. The Tejon Ranch, owned by the Chandlers, contains about 300,000 acres.

In recent years there has been a rush of motion-picture bigwigs to become landed gentry. When war taxes came on, many plunged into land purchases on which they could lose money for a number of years, in order to cut down their income taxes. They thought it would take years before

citrus orchards or breeding farms for race horses
or pedigreed cattle could work around to profit. But
the war brought such an influx of manufacturing
wealth, and of persons needing homes, that rising
land values and livestock prices only enriched
them more. All this contributed to hospitality less
dignified but even more ostentatious than that of
the days of the dons.

It was the motion-picture studios, for instance,
which invented the publicity stunt of inviting
newspaper men from all over the United States to
be guests at premières in such places as Dodge City,
Kansas; Santa Fe, New Mexico; Lincoln, Nebraska;
San Francisco, or Virginia City. For such affairs
special trains or planes might leave several key
cities on the east coast, the west coast, the northern
and southern boundaries. On one such trip there
were sixteen bedroom coaches in the train when it
pulled out of Los Angeles. There were also two dining cars, a lounge car in which one had only to
press a button and a porter would bring anything
one wished to drink or smoke or eat, and another
car turned into an old-fashioned Western barroom.
Every guest was given a sombrero worth several
dollars, a camera, a large silk neckerchief, a self-
sharpening pencil with which to take notes, a note
pad in a leather case, and a few other gadgets.
There were at least thirty really famous movie stars

and as many more lesser stars to lend glamour to the scene—and to make brief personal appearances on the platform whenever the train stopped in a town. There were also a few beautiful girls not connected with the picture industry, apparently invited merely as conversational entertainers. Two railroad executives personally conducted the tour, two or three authors of distinction were in the party, and there were at least a dozen nationally noted newspaper persons besides several hundred who were local celebrities.

When the train had crossed nearly half the continent it met another train, bringing similar guests from the East and South, and the two proceeded together into a little midwestern town. From mayor to street sweeper, every man in the town had raised whiskers and rigged up some sort of pioneer costume and was at the station to meet the train. The stars were paraded through the streets in old-fashioned horse-drawn vehicles. All that day they were entertained and exhibited their most charming behavior until the première that night was over. Then they relaxed, as many of their guests had done already. Some took in the town, others got up private parties in staterooms. There were three fierce fights on the train, one between one of the noblest Western heroes of them all and his lovely young wife, in which both got black eyes.

In recent years even movie hospitality has been out-dazzled by garment-industry hospitality. Just as motion pictures have attracted actors from all parts of the world, they have also drawn costume designers. Los Angeles factories which had begun by making overalls saw their chance to get some of the world's most famous designers to create styles for them, beginning with ranch and hunting costumes and by now including practically everything in sportswear, so that Los Angeles calls itself the world's capital of the sportswear industry. In 1946, the first all-Pullman, all-streamliner through train from New York to the Pacific Coast carried 150 Eastern fashion editors, trade-magazine representatives, and retail executives to Los Angeles as guests of one Los Angeles manufacturer of bathing suits. After a day or two in Los Angeles, they were taken on a chartered ship to Catalina Island, where they were feasted and wined while a group of models headed by Miss America demonstrated bathing suits priced as high as fifty dollars apiece. There were more than six hundred guests on that trip. Two days later a rival bathing suit manufacturer took most of those same editors and buyers on a four-day special train trip to the Grand Canyon, and similar affairs kept them busy for two weeks, winding up with a men's-wear display at Palm

Springs which lasted several days and was attended by several thousand guests.

Like the bringing of Arab royalty to this country as the guest of a California oil company, this was hospitality for a purpose, but it all ties up with the pattern established by the princely rancheros of arcadian days. They, too, according to Roger Sterrett, president of the Historical Society of Southern California, made a great display of hospitality in order to impress their visitors and put them under obligations, and behind the scenes there was much strategic effort to arrange marriages. When the plan was to marry off a certain member first, the rest of the family collaborated with wonderful teamwork to make the plan succeed. The twelve-year-old sister who wanted the fourteen-year-old sister married out of the way so she might have her chance was just as clever in her way as the garment salesman showing his line of goods.

But something has come down from the spacious days of abundance which makes all Californians, no matter where they came from, cherish the traditions of a hospitality that never had to count the cost. And after they have lived in California ten years, even though they still think of some distant state or country as "back home," they begin to look on it as their heritage.

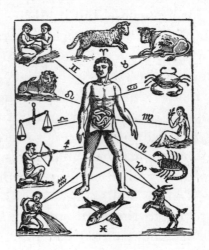

CALIFORNIANS are fond of short cuts to all their goals, including heaven. Especially in the southern half of the state, strange messiahs always have found a following, since it became Americanized. The first of them arrived in Los Angeles in 1852. His name was William Money, which gives ground for the assertion that thousands since then have come after Money. And an astonishing number of them have found a mighty good living. Many

[68]

of them have been involved in triangles, quadrangles, "octangles" and plenty of other tangles, but still devoted followers have been eager to give them their all.

Some have been sincere persons who believed they were guided by revelations, and some have established sects which have grown to national importance. Aimee Semple McPherson was one of the latter, and her Four Square Gospel now has followers in many states. Some others have been mere crackpots, mentally upset by their own interpretations of scriptural passages they did not understand. But so many have been simply fraudulent that in 1936 a special investigator, hired by the Ministerial Association of Los Angeles, declared that in that city religious impostors annually fleeced the public of far more money than was stolen by all the bandits, burglars, and confidence men. Among the cases he reported was one in which a "mystic" induced an aged woman to will him her home, valued at more than one hundred thousand dollars, on the promise that he would turn it into a temple to enlighten the world. That gift was voided without legal action by evidence that the woman was of unsound mind. Another was a case the investigator called attempted psychological murder. A seer who claimed power to read the future knew that one of his followers was greatly worried because he had heart disease. After several readings, the seer sadly and solemnly informed the worrier that he would die on a certain date and suggested ways in which he might dispose of his wealth before that date. The date set was only a few weeks away. The positive prediction preyed on the dupe's mind so that he began setting his affairs in order at once and suffered a heart attack which almost killed him within a week. When he keeled over the family called a doctor, not the seer, and when the doctor learned what was going on he called the investigator for the Ministerial Association. The result was that the seer left town hastily, and the patient lived on for a number of years.

But let's look at the more amusing side of this investigation. The law at that time forbade fortune telling but, in the effort to assure religious freedom, specified that its provisions should not interfere with the teachings of regularly ordained ministers. The result was ordination mills which would ordain anyone, sight unseen and by mail, for a fee. All kinds of commercial clairvoyants and fortune tellers immediately applied for ordination, for the certificates not only gave their holders authority to perform weddings, conduct funerals, and hold services but to ride on trains and busses for half fare. So many of those who obtained such "ordination" were fake palmists and clairvoyants that when the Ministerial Association decided to hire an investigator it secured Dr. U. L. DiGhilini, who had been stage manager for Anna Eva Fay, famous for her seances in theaters forty years ago. DiGhilini discovered that at least 918 persons had been ordained ministers or even bishops by one Los Angeles mill within the preceding twelve months and asked the editor of a New York magazine to publish an article exposing the racket. The editor couldn't believe the charges and the investigator offered to prove them by having the editor ordained a Doctor of Divinity for fifteen dollars or a bishop for forty dollars. He did those very things, but still the editor hesitated. After all, wasn't an editor a sort of minister, guiding the thinking of a flock? So DiGhilini wagered he could have Joe Penner's duck, Googoo, ordained. At that time Googoo was known, by picture or voice, to millions of American moviegoers and radio fans, and the editor couldn't believe that any creature so well known, and with such a funny name, would not at least make the "archbishop" who did the ordaining ask some questions. But only two days after the application was sent in a duly signed and sealed certificate, naming the Rev. Drake Googoo as a full-fledged minister, was returned to Penner.

For additional evidence, the investigator obtained ordination, from the same "archbishop," for "Nellie

Poorkluck," supposedly a Swedish servant girl from Minnesota. Nellie went to the city pound and liberated a stray dog. She cleaned it up, painted its toenails, and put an impressive collar on it. She explained to the "archbishop" that she had no money but would give her valuable dog for a certificate of ordination, and he made her a "reverend," too. For a third clincher, to prove that no references were looked up, the investigator got a friend to apply for a Doctor of Divinity degree, naming Eric Weiss as his sponsor. Weiss, who was "the Great Houdini," had been dead for many years. But the "archbishop" had such close contact with the other world that the ordination certificate came back by return mail. Evidently it took only a few minutes to check with the sponsor.

DiGhilini was respectful of all true spiritualists but publicly offered to duplicate any demonstration of occult powers by any "commercial" clairvoyant, frankly confessing he would do it all by trickery. The Authors' Club of Hollywood was one organization that asked for such a demonstration, and some of the things done in that performance would have seemed supernatural had he not assured those present they were not. A committee of fifteen of the most skeptical persons present was selected to stand on the stage and try to discover the trickery. That committee included Rupert Hughes, the late Irvin

Cobb, and several other persons of unquestioned
sincerity and curiosity, and the writer of this book.
Near the rear wall of the stage was a cabinet of
steel rods from which hung curtains. We commit-
teemen were asked to examine the front of the
stage to see there was no trap door there, and then
carry the cabinet out and place it on any chosen
spot. We did so, shaking out the curtains and throwing them up on top of the metal framework. Then
one of us brought an ordinary straight-backed
chair, and the young woman who was secretary of
the club sat in it. We tied her legs to the chair legs,
tied her hands together, made her bend so that her
elbows rested on her thighs, and sewed her sleeves
to her skirt. Then we let down the curtains. In the
front curtain were three slits. Some of us stood on
each side of the cabinet. We could see all around it
and over the top of it. Then through the slits pale
hands flung dewy-fresh carnations, one by one, into
the audience, until three dozen had been tossed out.
We had been there all the time, on a well-lighted
stage, and any one of us would have testified in
court that no flowers had been passed into the cabinet. Then we lifted the curtains again. The young
woman was just as we had seen her a few minutes
before, bound and sewed so she could not move
hand or foot.

At frequent intervals, for several months, the investigator gave public demonstrations of that kind, in an effort to teach Angelenos that apparent miracles were not necessarily proof of supernatural powers. But it didn't do much good. Preachers who had evolved their own systems of theology were on the street corners, on the bathing beaches, on the radio. Messiahs who knew just when the world would end, and whose followers would be the only persons saved, could always find adherents, some of whom were ready to sell their homes and other worldly goods and turn the proceeds over to their leaders. What need would they have of property if the world came to an end? Just what need the messiahs would have of it didn't seem to puzzle them.

Nothing seemed too fantastic. A Negro named Walker petitioned the court to change his name to Cassowary because he belonged to a sect in which every member had to have the name of a bird. At least he picked an unusual one. A bus driver went to court, alleging that a messiah had alienated not only his wife but his savings of one thousand four hundred dollars. A woman who went to a temple in which the crutches and wheel chairs of persons cured by faith were exhibited, was assured faith could heal her and turned over ten thousand dollars. A week later she was desperately in need of a surgical operation and asked for her money back, but the reply was that she had given it to the Lord and nothing could be done about it. The leader of a Mountain of God cult called himself "Son of God" and announced that the only safe place on the Pacific Coast would be his mountain ranch. The husband of one of his followers charged that the messiah had influenced his wife to desert him and their four children to go with him to the mountain. A Glendale woman, seeking annulment of her marriage to one messiah, revealed that he had used at least four aliases in his labors for the Lord. A suit for custody of a three-year-old child revealed that it had been born to a San Diego College co-ed who had been living in a "holy triad" with a sixty-year-old "Egyptian Coptic Priest" and his wife.

The Reverend Joe Jeffers had plenty of troubles for a number of years, but still appears to have plenty of followers. The Reverend Joe's churches have borne such names as the Kingdom Temple, the Temple of Jehovah and the Temple of Yahweh. The Kingdom Temple congregation ran into rough going after one couple in it sued for thirty-eight hundred dollars they alleged Joe had secured from them by fantastic promises, but once that little matter was settled Joe bobbed up again in his Temple of Jehovah. A reporter who called on him found him "living in luxury." He asserted he was a true messiah and regularly held two-way conversations

with God. When his wife divorced him, charging
acts unsuited to one of the Lord's anointed, he con-
veniently announced that Yahweh, the Great Spirit,
had forbidden him to pay alimony, but she attached
the funds of his current temple. In 1947, he found
it difficult to get a place for another temple and
moved to the suburb of Baldwin Park. Hardly had
his temple got going there when neighbors went to
court in an effort to have it declared a nuisance.
On top of that his ex-wife again haled him into
court for delinquent alimony, but no attachable
funds could be found. Joe testified that Yahweh was
holding a treasure of more than four hundred billion dollars in trust for him on Orion, but in assets
of this world he had only $1.53. He testified that
he could secure instantaneous contact with Yahweh. But no funds were forthcoming.

All these events have made headlines in Los
Angeles newspapers, but none has discredited Joe.
If today he should call on his flock to follow him to
an earthly heaven in the High Sierra, where moth
and rust do not corrupt and atom bombs cannot
break in and destroy—which is one of the timely
projects he has considered—there is little doubt a
long caravan of true believers would follow him.

Despite its endless chain of home-grown messiahs, Los Angeles is always ready to give a hearing
to outside talent. In 1947, Avak the Healer was im-

ported from Armenia to try to cure a wealthy young invalid at Palm Springs. Every day thousands of southern Californians made the long trip to the desert resort, on the bare chance of getting Avak to include their invalids in his prayers. No miracles were reported, and Avak got so worn out he looked as if he needed a healer himself. He went into retirement without doing anything that looked commercial. But a few months later plans for a temple of healing for him in Los Angeles were announced. "Physician heal thyself" is old advice, and Avak seemed bent on becoming well heeled.

Aimee Semple McPherson has left a more impressive monument to herself than has any other California leader who founded his or her own religious sect. Aimee's temple is a huge building. Nearly anyone in Los Angeles can tell you where it is, for nearly everyone has been there. In Aimee's time it was often said that it "put on the best show in town." The average service was a dramatic performance, with angels, shepherds, apostles, and others in costume, and Aimee always in the most striking and beautiful costume of them all. There were tableaux, and often as Aimee preached there was action to illustrate what was said. When the collection plate was passed, Aimee made it clear she expected folding money, not mere dimes and quarters and half-dollars, for the Lord needed a lot of money to feed the hungry and take care of those in trouble. And it must be said that a mere telephone call to Aimee's office, telling of a family in distress, usually brought a prompt response in the form of a big basket of groceries.

Aimee was always beautifully and tastefully dressed and artistically made up. She had a fine stage presence, and though her voice was a little shrill it had the exciting quality of shrill notes on a violin. As she told it herself, she was a girl of seventeen, who loved to dance and skate and had visions of going on the stage, when Robert Semple, an Irish evangelist, came to her town in Canada. "I went to scoff," she said. "I was inclined to atheism then. But he made such an impression I could not dance it off or skate it off. I went again and was converted."

She must have been a beautiful girl then. Semple went on to the next town, but the ardent young convert wrote him a letter which affected him so that he returned to see her. "So I became the evangelist's bride."

She toured with Semple in Canada, Ireland, and England, and then they went to China. There Semple died, and her daughter Roberta was born.

"When in doubt I always pray for guidance," she said. "I took the baby out to Robert's grave and knelt on it, asking a sign. The baby cried and I took that as an answer. We returned to America."

In Canada a big camp meeting was in progress. She went there, offering her services. They put her to washing dishes. She was only nineteen but she was alert. Soon she was playing the piano, then leading the choir. Then, when an exhorter's voice gave out, she preached and made people cry.

"A woman who heard me," she said, "asked me to go to her town and hold a meeting. I went, but there were only about twenty persons present. I couldn't stand that. Again I turned to prayer. I took a chair, carried it to the main intersection in the town, climbed on it, closed my eyes, and began to pray. I forgot everything but my prayer till I heard a man say: 'She's in a trance.' I opened my eyes and saw a crowd. Then I sprang down and cried: 'Follow me!'"

They followed her into the hall she had hired, and she preached. In three days she had to have a bigger hall. Small wonder that a girl who had such a grasp of a situation when she was nineteen had become a national figure in her latter thirties. She is credited with many miracles, including the one of walking miles across the desert without soiling her white satin shoes. She settled in Los Angeles in 1919 and in a few years had built a $1,500,000 temple seating 5,000 persons and had 16,000 names on the membership rolls of her congregation. She preached ten times a week, directed a Bible school with 1,200 students, and edited her church paper.

About 1924, it was announced that Krishnamurti, a Hindu boy who had been adopted by Dr. Annie Besant, was being hailed as the new messiah. Dr. Besant had been educating the boy to be "the perfect flower of Theosophical thought." As Madame Tingley had established an important Theosophical colony in San Diego, it didn't take Krishnamurti long to get to California, and by 1928 what was to be an annual theosophical encampment, drawing visitors from Australia, New Zealand, India, several countries of Europe, and many parts of America, was established at Ojai, with Krishnamurti as its star attraction. Krishnamurti was an olive-skinned, black-haired young man with enormous eyes. He spoke in parables. Unlike Aimee and the Reverend Joe, he lived with the utmost frugality and simplicity, and there was no showmanship about the gatherings. He was a courteous man who didn't tell anyone how to find salvation or peace—he said every man must find it for himself. "People are seeking happiness but ignoring truth, the only happiness," he said. "They are seeking candles and electric lights and ignoring the sunlight. What good can it do a man to spend the whole day in holy contemplation, and then be cruel to a little child? When you find truth you will not want any other man's possessions but will want to share with him your great possession."

People from near-by Santa Barbara, who had spent their lives piling up possessions, listened to such philosophy and sighed: "How true!" But they hung on to their possessions.

There is an important Theosophical center at Ojai, and thousands of the faithful visit it every year. Krishnamurti makes Ojai his part-time home. But he is no longer an out-and-out Theosophist. Like Aimee and many of the others, he wishes to be free from any secretarian rules in his pursuit of truth but, unlike most of them, he does not wish to lay down any rules for others. You can't help getting a lift out of a talk with him, even if you don't always know precisely what he means. He seems too sincere ever to think whether his views or his course are to his advantage or not.

If you asked a stranger his address, and he said "Holy City," you might think he was either joking or crazy. But Holy City, California, has been on the map quite a number of years. It is just off State Highway 17, between Santa Cruz and San Jose, and as you drive through it you think you are seeing things. The highway is lined with huge statues which look like Santa Clauses. Like many of the heavens now being suggested as atom-bomb shelters, Holy City was inspired by the appearance of Halley's comet in 1910. "Father" William E. Riker, who had been a showman, saw his chance to get hold of a few hundred acres of mountain land and become the high priest, political boss, and social dictator of it. By mixing economics and religion in about equal parts, he developed his own creed and found about seventy-five persons who liked it —and Holy City came into existence. For some time it had its own radio station, and so many listened to it that Riker was twice a candidate for governor on a "perfect government" platform. Indeed, all went well with him till, during the war, some of his antiwar sentiments were so vehemently expressed that he was arrested for sedition. The case was dismissed on grounds of religious freedom, but the route of the state highway was altered so that now Holy City is on a side road, thereby missing many tourist dollars.

Each of the Santa Clauses is set in a sort of shrine and is placarded in large letters with a message to the world. One declares that "Father Riker says Uncle Sam must take over all the banking business." Another demands free insurance and scientific management of unemployment and the business of all disabled persons. Another proclaims Holy City to be the Comforter and the New Jerusalem. Still another urges: "If you are contemplating marriage, suicide or crime, see me first." There is an information booth, the sign on which cheerfully promises: "All mysteries answered." One of "Father" Riker's publications is "Government Explained," and another is "White Man Supremacy."

"Father" Riker and his wife seem to be the only married persons in the group of adherents to his religious and economic theories.

From nudist colonies to swamis, southern California has all the cults you ever heard of and many which are purely local inventions. The climate and the millions of acres of sequestered mountain and desert land which can be leased or bought for very little have made that section inviting to nudist colonies, and by mixing a few religious teachings with their theories of health most of them manage to appease the local authorities for a while. But soon some fervent preacher of an opposing sect arouses opposition and compels their closing. Numerous newspaper reporters have visited nudist colonies, and none has reported seeing anything shocking. But it isn't always easy to shock a reporter.

Astrologers and mystics are the cultists who flourish longest and most profitably in California. If they are good looking, have pleasing personalities, and steadfastly predict the things their clients wish to hear, they are likely to become the fad of the moment. One famous actress once told me: "I'm always willing to spend a few dollars to hear some authoritative predictions which give me a lift. Whenever I hear of a new mystic who sounds good I call up Mary Pickford and some of the other girls and we try him out. We don't really believe them, but it sounds good." Miss Pickford, incidentally, almost started a cult of her own with her book *Why Not Try God?* It had a vast number of readers in California, and had she chosen to hire a hall or build a temple her fame and personal attractiveness would have drawn huge congregations, and her earnestness would have turned many of them into followers. But Miss Pickford was too much occupied with other affairs to consider such an effort.

Many persons famous in Hollywood won't sign a contract or engage in any business venture without first consulting a mystic. One Hollywood personality had a valet who was a handsome and clever fellow. When the valet saw how interested many persons with money to spare were in mysticism, he began reading up on the subject. His employer took him to Paris, where the young man began operating as an amateur mystic. He did so well that he set up in business for himself. When he returned to Hollywood he was "an internationally noted mystic," and even some of those who had known him as a valet were among his clients. He could appear before a woman's club and make a speech which so thrilled the ladies that afterward many of them would ask him for private appointments. He could coin beautiful platitudinous utterances and could make every receptive listener think she had wonderful possibilities if only she had the proper guidance from the stars. For some years he lived handsomely and got much newspaper publicity. But so many of his published predictions proved erroneous that his popularity waned and he moved to Nevada, where he used his mystic powers to pick race-track winners and advise clients how to beat the gambling games. Even there many of his clients were visitors from Hollywood, which likes to think of itself as "the most sophisticated spot on earth."

Besides all its queer sects and brand new diversions of theology, all the old established faiths flourish in Los Angeles. The First Congregational Church there boasts it is the biggest and busiest church in America, in point of persons served weekly. Besides its pastor, it keeps six or seven assistant ministers busy. Services, meetings, classes, forums, and other activities make up a schedule which keeps people flocking in and out of the edifice all day every day, and every evening, too. There are classes for blind persons, for young children, for young mothers. Every Sunday night there is a nonsectarian free forum, which has attracted many famous lecturers and has an average attendance of more than one thousand. In fact, all the churches are similarly busy, though no others engage in quite as many activities, which they consider outside their sphere.

But still a newspaper advertisement announcing that "Charlie, the entertaining evangelist," will preach, sing, and whistle at the Highway to Heaven Church brings a crowd to that institution, and the Church of the Open Door is sure of a good crowd when its advertisement announces that its minister will tell "Why No Atom Bomb Will Ever Fall on Los Angeles." Every Saturday the Los Angeles newspapers carry full pages of Sunday sermon announcements, though they limit the space so that all the announcements are in small type. A few of those advertisements may bring some readers more laughs than do the funny papers, but they bring crowds to the churches.

You can find queer cultists in the richest and in the poorest communities in southern California, and it would take keen judging to say which are the queerer. Most of what they say publicly is good for people to hear. Between them and the long-established sects, practically everyone is more or less exposed to moral guidance. In spite of that, Los Angeles is famous for strange and sadistic crimes.

It has been estimated that the fake religionists

alone—the fellows who got their Doctor of Divinity degrees for fifteen dollars—annually swindle Angelenos out of at least $1,500,000, besides all that is collected by sincere crackpots, barefoot prophets who think they see visions, and persons who think they can establish heaven on earth by means of weird combinations of economics and religion. Not all the residents of the City of Angels are sure of heaven, but there are very few who haven't bought some kind of ticket to it.

IT'S AN old California custom to put pleasure before business, or, at least, to make pleasure an essential part of the business of living. In most pioneering communities the dangers and hardships of existence tended toward austerity and economy. California's basic theory, according to Bancroft, was: "Pleasure, up to a certain point, must be classed among the utilities, as well as plowing and sheep raising, for without enjoyment the race would speedily deteriorate."

As soon as California got going, it was a land of riding, racing, dancing, hunting, cock fighting, bull-and-bear fighting, and sports challenging the most daring horsemen. Not only the vaqueros but every young blood in California became so skilled in the use of the *reata* that mere wild bulls hardly provided excitement enough, and they went forth to lasso elk and grizzly bears. Grizzlies which could kill a horse with a blow or a man with a single mighty hug were hunted by many an unarmed caballero, who was ready to battle man or beast with his trusty *reata*. Even when the Californians went into battle against General Kearny's tired army at San Pasqual—and gave it a pretty thorough whipping—many of them preferred their *reatas* to guns and lances, and the Americans feared them more. Being dragged into captivity by a *reata*, one end of which is attached to a saddle horn on a fast horse, is no fun.

Serenades under señoritas' windows were routine procedure. But it was more dramatic to drag a grizzly bear there, for daring was one of the things the señoritas liked most. If one caballero was serenading a señorita, his rival was not unlikely to show up with a lassoed grizzly. Thus many a serenader was forced to interrupt an impassioned song declaring his desire to die for his lady in order to run for his life.

[89]

John Bidwell wrote that the Americans had a saying that "the Spaniards"—all Californians were called Spaniards by the first settlers from the United States—"wouldn't do anything they couldn't do on a horse." And Walter Colton asserted that the reason fish were rarely seen on California tables was that fishing couldn't be done on horseback, but anything which could be done on horseback was eagerly adopted. There were so many horses on the ranchos, it was the custom for nearly every rider to lasso a different one every day, so that many would be more or less accustomed to being ridden. The inevitable result was that most of them were half wild, but that was tame enough. As soon as a boy was strong enough, he went into the fields, lassoed one of those half-wild horses, mounted it bareback, and let it run away with him till it was tired enough to be docile. The men even lassoed firewood to drag it to the big outdoor kitchens.

Such daily habits naturally led to a skill a man would enjoy showing off before the ladies, though some of the contests do not seem very ladylike. One was the *carrero del gallo*, in which a rooster was buried in sand so that only its head protruded. At a signal the horseman would ride at full speed from sixty yards away, swing low as he passed the fowl, and come up with its head in one hand. If he failed he was jeered.

Another game was a sort of drop-the-handkerchief on horseback. All the horsemen but one would form a ring with their horses' heads pointed inward. The other would ride around the ring, carrying a switch, or, rather, a good stout stick. When he thrust this into some other player's hand from behind, the race was on. The man with the stick endeavored to catch the other and whip him with the stick, pursuing him so closely he could not crowd into the place left vacant.

The bull-and-bear fight was another spectacle that was not for the lily-livered. The bull and the bear were tied together, the bull having one of its forelegs strapped and the bear one of its hind legs. The battle which ensued was gruesome and terrible, yet it was deemed something worth going miles to see.

There was much on the prettier side, however. Nearly every act of social life was accompanied by music. Every Californian seemed able to play the guitar without instruction. Even wash day was a fiesta. The laundry was allowed to accumulate for several weeks and then, instead of blue Monday, a gay party had a *marienda* beside some sparkling stream, with plenty of food and wine, which wound up in a dance. Walter Colton says: "The Cali-

fornians would hardly pause in a dance for an
earthquake, and would renew it before the vibra-
tions ceased. Even the mission Indians had a *baile*
every Saturday night, in which the girls did the
choosing of partners, that being the Indian custom."

Ana Begue de Packman resents the idea that the
early Californians did nothing but dance. She says
they had large responsibilities and were up early
to ride out over their ranches and see that all was
well. That is true, but the work was largely of a
supervisory nature, often comparable to that of the
business executive who leans on his golf club while
he and another executive sympathize with one
another over the difficulty of getting a full day's
work out of an employee nowadays. Colton loved
Californians generally. He and every historian who
has studied the arcadian era in California admires
them. Yet all agree they were ready to turn almost
anything into a fiesta. When a very unpopular new
governor arrived from Mexico, for instance, there
were fireworks and banquets and all kinds of celebrations in his honor—after which the celebrators
got busy to compel his retirement and, when he
was forced out of office, had fireworks and rejoicing
again. Even when Commodore Jones made his
famous mistake of raising the American flag too
soon in Monterey—a mistake he afterward repaired
by re-raising the Mexican colors—the settlement

was celebrated by general and reciprocal festivities. There was a brilliant ball on the "Savannah," Jones' ship, and the compliment was returned at the Customs House, on shore, which was a rather nice way to end hostilities. After the capture of Los Angeles by the Americans, the Californians were, at first, cold and aloof. They remained shut up in their houses and had as little to do with the invaders as possible. But when the American band went into the little plaza and serenaded the whole town they could not retain their hauteur long. After all, a serenade was part of their tradition. It was an offer of affection, an expression of a desire to become better acquainted, and courtesy demanded that such a gesture be responded to with courtesy. So the Angelenos dressed in their best and came out to listen and applaud.

The drinking habits of the Spanish Californians were simple and pleasant. The missions became famous for their wines and brandies, and, as the land grants were made, were able to supply all the *haciendas* with grape cuttings. Indeed, there was to come a time when the dread phylloxera destroyed the vineyards of France and nearly all the rest of Europe, and when cuttings from the vineyards of California were to revive the wine-making industry there. The making of grain alcohol was forbidden in those early days, and one suspects that

Harrison Rogers, quoted in a previous chapter, was mistaken when he said the padres at Mission San Gabriel gave him whisky to drink. Probably it was brandy. Even Richard Henry Dana, who spoke rather spitefully of California when he got the chance, said he saw no drunkenness in California.

But the Indians were no such sissies. They took to both wine and brandy with enthusiasm, and Bancroft reports they had a drink of their own, named pispipata, which was made of powdered calcined shells, wild tobacco juice, and wild cherries, powdered, shaken, and ground. Water was added till it assumed the consistency of a very thick paste. Sometimes corn or fruit of easy fermentation was used. "The drink," says Bancroft, "was equal to a mixture of rum, tobacco juice and opium. The horrible mixture prepared, the savages would seat themselves around it in the hot sun. Each, dipping a forefinger in the mess, would touch it to his tongue and give a smack of satisfaction. This done two or three times, the participant fell back dead drunk or dead indeed, if a little too much should be taken. It is said that during the lethargy induced the moderate participant seemed to realize the most ardent hopes indulged in while awake and, though his body was paralyzed, his soul entered the realms of superlative happiness."

Yet even that was not as deadly to the Indians as

was civilization. In 1770 there were 133,000 Indians in California, whereas the latest official count lists only 18,675. Nevertheless, it is best to give no specific proportions of the Indian drink, lest someone with more curiosity than brains attempt to produce it. The gentle and beneficent wine of the pastoral days, again according to Bancroft, was made thus: "Suitable ground was selected and a platform was placed thereon. This was covered with clean hides and grapes were piled upon it. Some well-washed Indians, having on only a zapata, the hair carefully tied up and hand-covered with cloth wherewith to wipe away the sweat, each having a stick to steady himself withal, were put to treading out the grape juice, which was caught in leathern bags. These were emptied into a large wooden tub, where the liquid was kept two or three months, under cover of the grape skins, to ferment. Such as did not flow off was put into wooden presses and the juice into copper jars, and covered with a kind of hat. Through two or three inserted tubes heat was conveyed to the 'mass to induce evaporation. Those jars served as a still for brandy. For white wine the first juice only was taken and stored."

If there should ever be another prohibition era, and one could get hold of enough clean hides and well-washed aborigines, that simple recipe might come in handy. It was good enough for some very good men. At San Jose, for instance, it is recorded that Padre Duran "was skilled in the pious industry of making brandy. His *aguardiente* was as clear as crystal or, when burnt sugar was added, became a clear yellow. It was double-distilled and was as strong as the good Father's faith."

As every *hacienda* raised grapes and made wine, and hospitality was the first law of the land, even the very temperate people their loyal descendants assure us all the early Californians were must have been a little high at times. Writing from San Jose, José Arnaz says: "The merrymaking sometimes took on the boisterousness of a frontier camp. Men would ride their horses up the steps of dancing pavilions and make them curvet on the floor. Women threw their rich embroidered China shawls, valued at three hundred pesos each, under the feet of dancers to serve as carpets."

San Jose and Los Angeles, incidentally, are the two cities in California which were founded. The other old towns began as military outposts, missions, or ranchos. It was after it was believed that the missions and the soldiers had made California, or much of it, safe for settlements not protected by soldiers that San Jose, Los Angeles, and Branciforte were founded. But some pretty dreggy humanity was gathered up for all these settlements, and the last named faded off the map long ago. Los Angeles, with a population now verging on two million, was founded by some eleven families, totaling forty-five persons—or a few less, according to some historians. Two or three babies born immediately before or after Governor Felipe de Neve formally founded the settlement may account for the divergence. To the credit of both communities be it said they quickly overcame their very bad beginnings. Writing of Los Angeles, Arnaz says:

"The residents, generally speaking, are very moral people, zealous in religious observance. One of their charming customs was to give thanks to God from their open windows at the break of day. One person would speak first, in a loud voice, and the rest would follow with responses." That salutation to the day, known as the alba, must have been practiced generally. Thus the day began with praise and singing, proceeded to the frequent accompaniment of music, and, whenever there was any excuse for it, wound up with a feast and a *baile*.

Every member of the family had a patron saint, whose day was a fete day. The fetes of *compadres* and *comadres* also were celebrated, and there were all the regular church holidays. La Noche Buena, or Christmas, for instance, was celebrated for fifteen days. If a family of twenty had forty *compadres* and *comadres,* it was also pretty sure to have a great many visitors, kinfolk, prospective kinfolk, or "tourists" from other ranchos, and it is easy to see that a continual round of entertainments would be imperative—anyhow, the Californians liked them.

California is so close to its past that many sprightly living persons have memories of it. Roger Dalton, present-day historian of the Azusa district, is the grandson of Henry Dalton, who became Don Enrique, married Guadalupe Zamorano, and was lord of a "little kingdom" of some seventy-two square miles. "There," writes Dalton, "except for the annoyance of an assessor who imposed and collected taxes, life was a round of endless joy." The land extended from the east city limits of Pasadena to the San Antonio Wash near Claremont. It was named the Azusa Dalton to distinguish it from the Azusa Duarte. The house was on an eminence in what is now the city of Azusa. Ordinarily friends and relatives came unannounced, except for the telltale squeaking of the *careta*. That squeak had one good feature in that when it was first heard it indicated that in two or three hours you would know who was coming. That gave the señora ample time to prepare bountifully for the expected guests. It was the custom to have a footman follow the lumbering *careta* with a pot of tallow. When the squeak got too bad the tallow-man would dash

up and pour tallow between the wooden wheels
and the wooden axle. This was how the *gringos*
came to call Mexicans "Greasers."

Describing a gathering at Christmas, Dalton
says:

"The señora had been keeping the neophytes
busy with preparations. She and her daughter-in-
law had been making tamales for the Christmas
dinner. The more or less responsible children were
kept busy stirring *conserva de calebasa* to keep it
from scorching. Sons and daughters with their
families were arriving from El Pueblo (Los
Angeles) which was thirty miles away and from as
far off as San Francisco. Don Enrique was on hand
to greet all comers but found it necessary to ride
off continually when the work was most threaten-
ing, to instruct his mayordomos or direct the Indians; then in again to tempt his guests with blends
he had concocted in his cellars."

Yet even the best and happiest of persons have
their little disagreements. The exuberant health
and spirits of the Californians seem at times to have
found expression in some robust fun. Alfred Robinson thus cited an incident:

"The usual season for '*Carnes tolendas*' is during
the three days previous to Ash Wednesday, but
here they commence two weeks earlier. Whilst

these amusements last, it is dangerous for one to go into a house where he is acquainted, for he is liable to be well drenched with Cologne or scented water. This is accomplished by the following preparatory process. As many eggs as may be required, are emptied of their contents, by perforating a hole at each end, through which they are blown by the mouth. The shells are afterwards immersed in a large basin of prepared essences, with which they are partly filled and the holes sealed with wax. Thus made ready, they are broken upon the heads of individuals. Oftentimes invitations are given for a select company to assemble at a specified place, when all attend at the time appointed 'armed and equipped' for a battle with the eggs. On such occasions, as the excitement grows warm, and their ammunition becomes nearly exhausted, they resort to wet napkins, which they slap at each other. From these they have recourse to tumblers of water; from these to pitchers, and from pitchers to buckets, until, tired and exhausted by the exercise, they desist.

"During the continuance of a certain marriage festival, one of these frolics was held at the house of the bride. Among the persons invited were the Padres Antonio and Menendez; at the close of the evening, when *buckets* were in constant requisition, the two friars became heated, and attacked each other with floods of water. Menendez, the weaker of the two, retreated to an adjoining dormitory and closed the door. Padre Antonio, urgent to follow up the attack, pursued him; when Menendez, seeing no means of escape, seized from beneath the bed an article, oftener used than mentioned, and let it fly, contents and all, full into the face of Padre Antonio, who had just appeared at the door. The consequences were the loss of two of the poor friar's front teeth, and a conclusion of the *fun*."

It may have been because some celebrants got out of hand that way that even a lover wishing to serenade a lady had to have a license in early-day Los Angeles. It is on record that one who played and sang very badly was fined, not for serenading but for doing it unmusically. Ah, if such a Daniel could only sit in judgment on some of the radio programs of today!

It is an interesting fact not generally known in California that much of what is called Spanish cookery there is of Indian origin. The wife of the owner of a "Spanish restaurant" in San Gabriel visited Spain a few years ago and found that the Spaniards knew nothing of tortillas, tamales, frijoles (beans), as the Mexicans cook them, and other foods common to the "Spanish" restaurants of California. In fact, she says that when she went to Stockholm, later in the same tour, she found the Swedes better acquainted with some of those dishes than the Spaniards were, for the sea-faring Swedes had picked up many recipes which fitted in well with ship cookery. Corn, beans, rice, and garbanza peas are all native to Mexico and had to be introduced into Spain. "Jerky," or dried meat, was also of Indian origin. The Indians ground corn with their *metates*, added jerky and chile peppers, garlic, onions, and other native herbs. The seed of the purple sage, wild grapes, blackberries, gooseberries, water cress and several other greens were also native, and the plains Indians dried many of them.

The rancheros had only a light breakfast on arising but returned at nine o'clock for the *almuerzo*, consisting of chile-flavored sausages, fried beans, tortillas, sweet curd cheese, red wine, and, when it was obtainable, coffee. When the mid-day angelus sounded they stopped work, wherever they were, to bow their heads in thanks for having been sustained so long on such scanty rations and then rode home for a lunch of broth, meat and vegetables something like the New England boiled dinner, pigweed salad, tortillas, red wine, or coffee. And fried beans, of course, "beans, more beans and warmed-over beans being the order of every day," according to Mrs. de Packman. From dawn to night, there was never a meal without them. After that they took a siesta and didn't eat anything till the *marienda,* which was afternoon tea in the home, though it was the word for a picnic when outdoors. That collation was often only herb tea (yerba buena or some other wild herb) and little cakes, or a cooling drink made of orange-blossom wine, *chia,* and sweetened water, served with *tostados* (crisp corn wafers) and *conserva* (preserved fruit).

Having held back thus all day, the ranchero had to have a really substantial dinner, especially if he had honored guests, which usually he did. Mrs. de Packman gives us this account of a real *boda,* or formal dinner.

"The guests approaching announce themselves, calling out: 'Hail, gracious queen!' *El patron* and his household in chorus respond: 'Through the glory of God granted.' 'Come in, come in, my good friends!' urges the patron. 'Fortunate are the eyes that look upon you!'

"With open arms the patron greets his guests and leads them in and the men drink toasts to the ladies with much ceremony while saying: 'I extend my arm. I crook my elbow. By all the living saints, to our hostess!' and then, 'I drink to all.' "

Then came the servants with filled dishes, and here is a sample menu:

Chicken meat-ball soup
Tongue salad and toasted red chile sauce
Roast fowl drenched with red chile sauce
Young chicken stewed with rice and served
with tomato and green chile relish
Leafy green salad
Tamales and enchiladas
Beans
Tortillas
Red wine and white wine
Turnovers, buns, shortbreads, and fruit dainties
Candied pumpkin   Boiled custard
Angelica wine

Maybe it isn't such a wonder that, thus fueled up, they could dance for two or three days and nights. Nor is it surprising that General Vallejo, for whom the city of Vallejo is named, needed fifty house servants.

That gives an idea of the simple, gay, hearty, and abundant life the Americans found when they flooded into California following the war with Mexico. It was a life born of the wealth and prodigality of nature, the abundance of products of the soil. The Americans tried to outdo it with the splendors money can buy, as, suddenly and unexpectedly, the wealth of gold and silver turned bartenders into magnates, pick-and-shovel men into lords of palaces, and at least one humble river-boat clerk into the most fabulous banker in American history, but theirs was a frenzied splendor and a spurious glory as compared to the pastoral days.

The gold rush started by James Marshall's discovery in 1848 revealed the Mother Lode region as the greatest gold-producing region in history up to that time, but the Comstock Lode a few years later was producing so much silver that half the world went mad. Yerba Buena, a village of only twelve houses in 1844, became San Francisco, financial center of the gambling world. Ralston the Magnificent became the wizard staid bankers in London looked to as the greatest genius of their age. Between 1860 and 1876, San Francisco was so bedazzled by its own glitter that every night there were a hundred Belshazzar's feasts.

From its earliest days, California was used to strange visitors about whose past it knew nothing, but if their manner was *caballero*, or gentlemanly, it accepted them at face value. That was the rule in *California de antes*, or California before the Americans came, and it must be confessed that many of the Americans themselves were such swaggering, lawless fellows they had no right to draw the line against anyone. Thus, in the early days of United States rule, all men who appeared to be manly, even if they were pretty tough customers, were accepted and admired, and all women of any sort whatever were welcomed.

It is history that several times when a reform movement struck one town, causing it to round up all its prostitutes and ship them to another, the second community met them with a brass band.

Not only a wide variety of men, from a wide variety of races, but an equally varied assortment of women were attracted by the Gold Rush. One of them was Lola Montez, an Irish girl who became the mistress of the King of Bavaria and almost caused a war. Like many another person in Europe, she heard of the Gold Rush and when she had to get out of Bavaria, it was San Francisco, not Paris or London or Rome, for which she headed.

All the first mining had been placer mining. In 1850, a man named George McKnight, plodding through an area known as Grass Valley, stubbed his toe. No doubt George cursed, as most men do when they stub their toes, but something went flying out in front of his hobnailed boot. Kicking a chunk of rock loose from the mother rock was something unusual, and George picked it up to look at it. It was quartz and it was full of gold. That was the beginning of hard-rock mining in California. The town of Gold Hill sprang up, a tent village at first and a very crude town at best, but millions of dollars were taken out of Gold Hill.

Lola Montez landed there in 1853. She arrived with a pet bear on a chain, a basket of champagne, doubtless the gift of some San Francisco admirer, and such a glittering assortment of clothes as Grass Valley had never imagined. She took the biggest house she could get and immediately began to give parties like none Grass Valley had ever seen, showing no more perturbation over a little scandal than she would have shown in a court of Europe.

One who looked on Lola Montez as a fairy godmother was a little girl named Charlotte Crabtree. Her mother, Mary Anne Crabtree, had come out from New York and was running a boarding house. As a child of six Charlotte, or Lotta, had learned to sing "Annie Laurie," but when asked to sing it in a San Francisco school had burst into tears. That had been shortly before Mary Anne Crabtree moved to Grass Valley.

Lola Montez liked the little red-haired girl, made a pet of her, taught her to dance, gave her confidence, and took her to a camp known as Rough and Ready, where Lotta danced on an anvil. The miners roared approval of the child, and that start at Rough and Ready began the career of as famous and as popular an actress as America ever produced. Many "first ladies of the stage" shone like rockets for a while and are now forgotten, but Lotta Crabtree is part of Western history. She will live in tradition and romance when many an artist the critics classed as far greater has faded into oblivion.

But this chapter is about the social ways and manners of California, and perhaps nothing indicates the standards of Grass Valley better than this incident: Every California community which gave promise of permanence had its newspaper, and Grass Valley was no exception. One editor of the Grass Valley Telegraph either had come from more prudish surroundings or was hurt because his lady friend had not been invited to one of Lola Montez' parties. Either of these circumstances might make an editor feel it his duty to speak out against anything which might tarnish the high moral record of his town. Anyway, that editor of the Telegraph felt it his duty to speak of Lola Montez in a manner she felt was slanderous. She promptly went to his office and horse-whipped him. The sympathies of the community were wholly with Lola. The unwritten law of those early American days was that anyone's private affairs were his own, so long as he did not make them a public nuisance. The editor left town the next day and shortly afterward committed suicide.

There is one story of American sportsmanship in the Mother Lode country which is brightly to the credit of the swashbuckling Forty-niners. One of the miners who went to the gold-rush town of Weaverville was John Carr, a blacksmith. Blacksmithing proved so profitable that soon Carr was able to leave his shop in charge of an assistant and go east to bring out his wife. He left a few straggly huts and tents. When he returned a year later, Weaverville was a thriving town of two thousand, and lots one could have had for nothing when he left were selling at eight hundred dollars apiece. But women were still rarer than gold. Carr brought back with him not only his wife but his brother's wife and another man and his wife. The arrival of three women at one time threw Weaverville into ecstasies. It was decided to honor them with a ball. Tickets sold for ten dollars each. Carr records the ball as a historic event, at which "more boiled shirts were worn . . . than ever before at Weaverville." But that was because most of them were seen repeatedly. The men owning them were generous. Shirts were swapped all night long, so that practically every man had at least one dance in genteel costume.

Thus the resourcefulness of the Yankee who would not be denied his fun was grafted on a Spanish culture which looked on pleasure as an essential part of living. And the combination has not been too bad.

California has never lost the fiesta spirit of its youth. Probably no other state has nearly as many

annual pageants and celebrations of historic anniversaries. The Santa Barbara Fiesta annually
brings out heirloom costumes, heirloom vehicles,
laces, shawls, and manners. Hundreds of the finest
horses in America, wearing silver saddles worth
many thousands of dollars apiece and bearing
caballeros who look like conquistadores, even
though their names are Murphy, Mitchell, or something else wholly un-Spanish, parade the streets.
Stagecoaches scarred by bullet and arrow carry
lovely ladies wearing high combs and mantillas.
The Mission Play at San Gabriel ran continuously
for more than twenty seasons, till depression forced
its discontinuance, and has had several revivals
since. The Pilgrimage Play, just over the hill from
Hollywood Bowl, also is more than old enough to
vote. Hollywood Bowl is one place in which a symphony orchestra of more than one hundred fine
musicians can play a whole season at a profit, as an
audience of twenty thousand persons is not much
more than average. These "symphonies under the
stars" are possible because southern California
rarely has rain between May and October. The Bohemian Grove high jinks near San Francisco annually draw notables from all parts of the United
States, as do the annual celebrations of Rancheros
Visitadores and the De Anza Riders. And San Francisco and San Diego are always ready to put on an

international exposition at the drop of a hat. Between 1948 and 1954 practically every town in the Mother Lode area will celebrate a centennial and try to make the Gold Rush live again. Cherry-blossom festivals, almond-blossom festivals, grape festivals, pioneer days celebrations, and many others are as firmly established as is the world-famous Tournament of Roses in Pasadena. The old days are gone, but California not only has its bright memories but puts its Hollywood make-up men to work on them to make them seem more picturesque, more romantic, and more resplendent than they ever were. Time cannot fade nor custom stale their infinite variety, for every Californian who isn't an art director thinks he should be one, and tries his hand at some local historical pageantry.

IT WASN'T all for king, for country, or for God that the first bold adventurers overcame incredible hardships and conquered range after range of giant obstacles to get to California. It was to search for gold. Like the present, the sixteenth century was an age when vast numbers of persons were ready to believe anything. They thought the Fountain of Youth burst from the breast of Mother Earth instead of seeking it at the vitamin counter or the cosmetics counter, but even the most absurd radio commercial of today could have found its quota of believers then, so they must have been just as gullible and unsophisticated as we are.

Early in the sixteenth century, other legends as fairy-like as that of the Fountain of Youth were current in Spain. One was of an island in the west which was populated with amorous amazons who were rich in pearls and gold. Another was of the Seven Cities of Cibola, which also were treasuries of gold and jewels. Bernardo de Alarcón, first white man to set foot on California soil, in 1540, was looking for Coronado, who had gone before him to look for the Seven Cities of Cibola. Baja California was supposed to be an island from 1542 to 1701, when Father Eusebio Franciano Kino, following the Colorado River to its mouth, discovered it was attached to the mainland.

Every soldier and sailor had heard reports of the gold of the Incas in Peru and legends of the isle of amazons and the Seven Cities. Undoubtedly it was the will-o'-the-wisp of dazzling riches which led men to gamble their lives on ventures which today seem beyond human capabilities. All Joaquin Miller wrote of the daring and fortitude of Columbus, when he braved the unknown to find a new world, can be doubled in picturing the marches through trackless deserts and over mighty, repelling ranges.

There were savages, hunger, and thirst to battle and the continual recurrence of mirages which faded like dreams, giving place to heartbreaking reality. Moreover, Columbus sailed and sailed but never had to sail around the Horn in his flimsy craft.

The legend of the Seven Cities of Cibola is evidence of how our folklore colors our thinking and our beliefs. It was not of Indian or American origin. According to Dr. Frederick Wedd Hodge, it was an old Spanish tale, more or less involved with the stories of the lost Atlantis. When the Moors invaded Spain, seven Spanish bishops were said to have fled to Antilia, a group of islands somewhere to the west. There each of them became the ruler of his own city, or his own island, and the fortunate cities were shining things of gold and jewels.

Probably every child in Spain heard such legends, just as every child in America hears of Cinderella. In Mexico every adventurer saw himself as the hero of some such tale, just as most of us today get a vicarious thrill out of reading romances, and what was told about many a campfire as wishful thinking was reported somewhere else by an ear-witness who "heard it himself."

Thus stories went through Mexico that somewhere to the north lay the Seven Cities of Cibola. How they had changed from islands to oases in the desert was not explained, but why worry about a minor detail like that? In 1529, Nuno de Guzman headed an expedition into what are now Arizona and New Mexico to find them.

They found nothing but desert but brought back exciting stories of what the Indians said lay behind it. In 1536, Cabeza de Vaca and his followers determined to find the Seven Cities. De Vaca had already done a marvelous thing. He had led an expedition overland from Florida to the west coast of Mexico. Nuno's explorers had brought back tales of four-story and five-story palaces, which they had never seen and the Indians who told about them had never seen. The Indians in their way were as great at gossiping as anyone who starts neighborhood rumors. Tribes near and far had heard of the homes of the Cliff Dwellers, and doubtless many of them spoke as authoritatively of those places they had never seen as many of us do today of countries we have never seen. When one has a listener who is eager to hear fabulous tales, one is inspired to do one's best, and the eager questioning of the Spaniards, who were sure the treasure troves of the Incas were duplicated somewhere near, practically demanded directions to them. The accommodating Indians reported the wildest rumors they had heard, and Cabeza went forth, confident that he would wring the secret out of more distant Indians.

But all he did was spread the legend of the Seven Cities through many Indian tribes so that they, too, began to believe in them. If the white demigods were so sure there were seven cities of gold and jewels, it must be so.

After two swaggering expeditions had failed, the head of the Franciscans in New Spain was asked to send friars out to convert the Indians, perhaps with the idea of making them more truthful and accelerating the search. Two padres traveled eight hundred miles, baptizing many Indians but finding no shining cities. Father Marcos de Niva led another expedition in 1530, which brought back such glowing stories of things it had not seen that the viceroy accused the padre of relying on his imagination for his facts. But the Spaniards wanted to believe them. Pizarro had found treasure in Peru. Cortez had found it in the palace of the Montezumas. The Conde de Mont Errey had found it in what now is Monterrey, Mexico. But the Seven Cities of Cibola had not yet been found and must be found. Even those who knew that the legend of the Seven Cities antedated the discovery of America accepted it as prophecy, as inspired and almost as authoritative as Holy Writ.

That was why Francisco Vasquez de Coronado, governor of New Galicia, made one of the world's historic marches. He set out from Culiacan, now capital of the Mexican west-coast state of Sinaloa, and marched through what now are Arizona, New Mexico, and Colorado and into Kansas. When the Indians were friendly he was sure he soon would reach his goal; when they were hostile he was sure it was because they were defending the riches he sought.

Ahead of him went a Negro named Estaban, who continually sent back word of cities, greater than the city of Mexico, in which the palatial houses were filled with golden vessels and the people wore golden ornaments—including golden sweat scrapers! They were said to wear fine clothing and sleep in beds with sheets, and all the unofficial reports indicated that Estaban tried many of the beds.

Estaban had convinced the Indians guiding him that he was invincible and could lead them across the world, and he seems to have collected some of the handsomest women as he went along. But the last word was that Estaban had been killed, and his party was in flight. Coronado's expedition was on the march two years.

Yet the men who found gold in California were not looking for it. When James Wilson Marshall picked up a nugget in 1848 the whole world heard of it, but the Californians had discovered it long before that. They simply didn't get excited about it.

In 1842, Francisco Lopez, *mayordomo* at San

Gabriel Mission, was rounding up stray horses in Placerita Canyon, near Los Angeles, and casually pulled up a wild onion. Presumably he was going to munch it, for he rubbed the dirt away from its roots, and clinging to them he saw a little nugget of gold. That same year, Abel Stearns of Los Angeles, one of the *gringos* who weren't supposed to meet any of the señoritas, who had married Arcadia Bandini and become the richest man in southern California, wrote in his diary: "On Nov. 22, 1842, I sent to Alfred Robinson, Esq., 20 oz., California weight, of placer gold, to be forwarded to the United States Mint in Philadelphia for assay." Some years ago, Guy Giffen, associated with San Francisco's famous Pioneer Society, published a pamphlet citing evidence that for several years before 1848 gold was being sent out of Los Angeles for refining, and the chances are that some was sent to Mexico City before any was sent to the United States Mint. John Bidwell says that in 1841 one Baptista Ruelle found gold in the vicinity of Los Angeles. And José de Jesus Pico wrote: "To several of us, Father Luis Martinez, in 1829, gave gold: To myself, Raimundo and Gabriel de la Torre and Francisco Soto, he made a present of about 20 ounces of gold, not coin but in little balls, because of his affection for us who had been his pupils here in the Mission [San Luis Obispo]." General Vallejo says that gold was found as early as 1824, and that the failure of the Californians to search for it was due to "the tenacious resistance of the Indians of the Sierra."

Yes, plenty of Californians—even Americans who had become Californians—knew there was gold in California but didn't go mad. And maybe they were wiser than the new, un-Californianized Americans who began to come in after the war with Mexico, for California never was the same after their coming.

On January 24, 1848, Marshall was building a sawmill for John Augustus Sutter at Coloma when he picked up a piece of rock and saw it was not rock, but gold. That started the Americans rushing to all the creek beds and river beds, and it seemed that all of them were full of gold. The news spread around the world and caused such a widespread epidemic of greed as the world had never seen. Puritans and prostitutes, noblemen from Europe and convicts from Australia, Chinese, who heard of it because the miners sent shiploads of laundry to the Orient, and adventurers from South America —all found ways to get to California, and from all parts of the United States came a migrant horde. The fever which made them thirst for sudden wealth was in their blood and made them reckless, daring, and dangerous. San Francisco, which had been Yerba Buena till 1847, became the seaport for which ships of all nations headed. When they got there, crews deserted them to search for gold, and hundreds of deserted ships lay in the bay. Soldiers deserted Fort Mason to become miners, and Lieutenant William Tecumseh Sherman feared to pursue them far lest all the pursuers desert, too. From a population one historian says did not exceed sixty in 1846, San Francisco grew into a roaring city in a few years, and Sacramento, main supply base for the miners, bulged the hundred thousand mark. Drinking, gambling, fighting, murdering, stealing were the order of the day and doubly the order of the night.

Yet Phil Townsend Hanna, in *California Through Four Centuries*, says that invasion gave a needed tonic constituent to the lethargic culture then existing. "In the days of the Gold Rush," he writes, "no coward started for California and no weakling ever got there."

Courage has so much to do with all we admire and yearn for that even raw and brutal courage is far better than none. The courage of the new Californians was the kind that would demand and die for its rights and would not accept mere politeness as a substitute. In Spanish days any governor or alcalde could count on an important following if he was *muy caballero*, or very gentlemanly, and a favorite story was that Augustin Machado, having ridden in from his rancho to trade with a ship, was about to ride off with the goods he had selected, leaving the sordid detail of payment to be settled later over a friendly glass, when the supercargo demanded surety. Pulling a hair from his beard, Machado said haughtily: "Here! Deliver this to your captain and tell him it is a hair from the beard of Augustin Machado!" One doubts that Machado could have got away with that in Hangtown or Angels Camp or Rough and Ready. The men who poured into the Mother Lode Country demanded the gold, not the glitter, and knew that all their fellows were after the same thing and half of them didn't care how they got it.

To give a rough, unscientific idea of it, the Mother Lode was one of Nature's treasure troves of a few million years ago. It was a belt of gold about three hundred miles long that was hidden for aeons in the heart of the earth. Then came the squeeze which created the Sierra Nevada, and the belt was lifted up with it. For perhaps a million years the rains and melting snows had been washing down fragments of that gold till it impregnated the whole Sacramento Valley.

Hangtown, only a few miles from Coloma, was the first gold center. When the Forty-niners roared in, Hangtown grew so fast they didn't take time to name it. Everyone was out in the stream beds, panning out gold. One night a Frenchman named Cailloux waked to see three men rifling his poke. One held a knife to his throat and ordered silence. But next day Cailloux told, and that same day a posse from the south, pursuing three horse thieves, rode into the settlement. When the horse thieves were captured it was decided it was they who had robbed Cailloux, too, and they were hanged from a big oak branch which stretched out over the town's one street. That gave Hangtown its name, which stuck till 1854, when it was officially changed to Placerville. At that time only San Francisco and Sacramento outranked Placerville in population, and in all southern California, which now has a population of about five million, there were only about five thousand white persons.

This method of dealing out impromptu justice, or an acceptable substitute for it, became a California custom of the Gold Rush days. And names comparable to Hangtown became almost a habit. Some of the others given to communities by the devil-may-care miners were Pinch Em Tight, Dogtown, Grizzly Flat, Betsyville, Flea Town, Mosquito Alley, Milk Punch, Drunkards Bar, Bear Gulch, Whiskeytown, and Poker Flat. There still is conflict between the people of Shasta County and the federal government over the name of Whiskeytown. The historically minded residents insist on calling the town Whiskeytown, but the Post Office Department insists that mail to it be addressed to Schilling, one of several names given it after the first refusal of the postal authorities to sanction Whiskeytown.

Not all the Gold Rushers were on a physical and mental spree. One young fellow who arrived in Hangtown was a carpenter, who decided it would pay him better to build wheelbarrows than to mine gold, for wheelbarrows were in tremendous demand. He did so well he was able to go home and start a wagon factory, which he later turned into a great automobile plant. His name was John Studebaker. Another young fellow started a men's store in Hangtown and so prospered that he was able to go into the hat manufacturing business. His name was John B. Stetson.

Even clergymen joined the Gold Rush. The Rev. James Welch Brier, his wife, and three small sons were in the party that blundered into Death Valley.

Gold was what the miners wanted, to spend for whisky, wheelbarrows, overalls, hats, or the favors of the ladies, and a town by any name smelled sweet if it yielded gold. Hangtown yielded seventeen thousand dollars in one week when it was a brand-new camp. One pan yielded fifteen hundred dollars and the miners grew weary of washing out riches. American Bar yielded three million dollars in a short while. Some Mexicans took two hundred thousand dollars out of Bear Gulch in four days. Poker Flat yielded seven hundred thousand dollars in a month. In Ophir, the owner of a lodging house spent his spare time digging under it, and the dirt yielded one hundred dollars a day in gold dust. One strike in Onion Valley yielded six thousand dollars in an hour, including a single nugget worth eighteen hundred dollars. A man named Jenkins had a claim near Auburn. To work faster he conducted water from a near-by spring. The flow stopped, and he went to investigate. He found that the water was running into a gopher hole and shining with coarse gold when it emerged. In a month he washed out forty thousand dollars and then left for his old home state, feeling that a forty-thousand-dollar fortune was enough for anyone. There should be a monument to that man, perhaps the wisest ever in the Mother Lode country. Gold Hill yielded more than four million dollars, Weaverville thirty thousand dollars a week, and so one could go on for pages. It seemed that any man who wished to do so could wash a good living out of nearly any creek bed, and many could find riches there.

Yet human nature is such that as soon as most of those argonauts got hold of gold dust they wanted to gamble for more, or go in for wild excesses. For one man like Bret Harte, who became a shotgun messenger on a stage coach, there were fifty who thought the only thing money was for was to be squandered on loose living, and many a shameful impulse turned into a bloody blot on history. Near Weaverville, an entire Indian village was wiped out; more than 150 men, women, and children were massacred and only two baby girls spared. Mokelumne Hill boasted a record of five murders a week for seventeen consecutive weeks and never failed to have one on Saturday night.

Yet when the women of Mokelumne Hill expressed a desire for a church, possibly so that some who were getting old enough to reform could be married with propriety, the miners passed the hat and soon had enough gold dust and nuggets to build it.

Descendants of the Forty-niners like to put on red shirts, symbolic of the red undershirts the miners wore, and celebrate certain anniversaries in connection with the Americanization of California, but it cannot truthfully be claimed that the Forty-niners as a class contributed much more than daring, population, and wealth. It is significant that of the forty-nine men who drew up the constitution of California as a state in the United States, only eight were Forty-niners. The others had settled in California because they loved the land and its ways, not because of gold. The miners tore up the stream beds and turned them into heaps of mud and gravel.

They slaughtered noble forests without a thought of what they were doing to the country. They plundered ranches, killed cattle, invaded private property, and spread over the countryside like a devastating scourge, justifying themselves with the comforting thought that anything they did to the Californians, the Indians, or the Chinese was all right. There were plenty of splendid exceptions, but the main virtue of tens of thousands of them was an intrepidity, a fortitude, a defiance of danger, and a reckless readiness to tackle the impossible which time has refined in California's blood stream as the gold from the High Sierra has been washed clean in a thousand streams flowing down from it.

No rumor was too wild to start a gold rush in those swashbuckling days, and to this day many of the legends lure prospectors to barren and inaccessible deserts or mountain fastnesses. Mount Disappointment, on which the Los Angeles Times experimented with television in 1947, got its name from a story that still persists. One Saturday night an Indian entered a Los Angeles saloon, when Los Angeles still was a town of about two thousand, dropped a bag of gold on the bar, and called for drinks for all. The crowd responded willingly, trying to get the Indian so drunk he would tell where he found the gold. When he left, men tried to follow him, but the Indian eluded them. The next Saturday the Indian appeared in the same saloon with more gold. This time his pursuers followed him through what is now Pasadena and on up into the mountains, but again he vanished around a turn in the trail. The third Saturday night they followed the Indian to the peak now named Disappointment, when once more he vanished into the woods as if by magic. That angered them so that the noble fellows felt the Indian wasn't playing fair with them, and next time they saw him they gave him his choice of leading them to his gold mine or going to the happy hunting grounds. The Indian still proved uncommunicative, so they shot him. That may be just a story, but they still search for gold on Mount Disappointment, hoping to find the Indian's mine.

There are plenty of stories of heroism and nobility, too. What William Louis Manly did for the party lost in Death Valley is one of the most chivalrous and heroic stories of American history. Three groups of Forty-niners, numbering about one hundred men, women, and children, had marched for eighty days before they got into the valley. Even those who today ride into it on a smooth motor road can imagine they have entered the jaws of death. It is walled by high mountains and so strewn with boulders there is no place any kind of team or wagon could go over the mountains except on the few roads. Then there were no roads—and these travelers were driving ox teams. Weak from a shortage of food and water, they could not find ways of lifting the wagons over boulders as big as houses. They were hundreds of miles from civilization.

Some of the stronger single men determined to push ahead. Thirteen of them died in the effort, and it took the survivors forty days to reach safety. After four teamsters had left the party in that way, Manly went after them. When he overtook them they were in the camp of others who had gone ahead, begging for the entrails of an animal which had been killed. It was no use trying to take them back, and Manly went on with a man named John Rogers. It was a big day for them when they shot a crow and ate it, for there was no game in the desert.

After weeks they got to San Fernando Mission, weary and half-starved. But after only one day's rest, Manly and Rogers started back with a pack train of supplies. Even then it was such a hard trip back that they had only one little mule left when they got there. The desert is almost as trackless as the ocean, and when one has to climb ten-thousand-foot mountains and then descend into below-sea-level deserts, with no roads, trails, or discoverable passes, it takes a long time and is hard on man or beast. Not many men would have gone back after such a trip, as Rogers and Manly did. But they felt that if they did not go no one else could find the way or would endure the hardships to get there.

Another incident shows of what stuff Manly was made. In eastern San Bernardino County one may see the Alvord Mountains. In 1861, Charles Alvord, a noted prospector, led a party of Mormons into Death Valley in search of a lost cliff of silver. Asahel Bennett also was a leader of the party. When they could not find the lost mine, the party abandoned Alvord in the valley. On the way out they met Manly, who felt they should return, and Bennett and a man named Twitchell guided him back. They found Alvord camped on the west slope of the Panamint Mountains. In that country, if a man had a mule there was hardly anything for the mule to eat or drink and nothing for the man to eat but the mule, and if he ate the mule he would be likely to die of thirst and starvation before he could walk to any human habitation. Maybe Bennett and Twitchell went back to see if Alvord had found his silver cliffs after all. At any rate, when they found him he was in very poor physical condition, and they did not have enough supplies to carry four men to safety. So Manly stayed there to take care of Alvord while Bennett and Twitchell went back for more supplies. They never returned. But a Dr. George, leading another party, found Manly and Alvord and got them out of the desert.

The vision of lost mines is like Coronado's vision of the Lost Quivera. The next year, Alvord went back to Death Valley, looking for his lost ledge of silver, and has never been heard of since.

That is only one of hundreds of stories of lost mines for which thousands of men have searched in the course of years. The famous Death Valley Scotty was supposed to have found one of them. The fact seems to be that the whole Scotty legend was a hoax. But that, dear reader, will be reserved for another chapter.

It is an interesting fact that about May 1, 1947, there was a silver strike in the Panamint Mountains not far from where Alvord camped. At least it was close enough, as distances go in California, to revive the old legends.

In desert and mountain areas the old prospector, shabby, grizzly, but still with an unquenchable gleam in his eyes, is a familiar sight. From the Borrego Valley of eastern San Diego County to Shasta County, more than a thousand miles away by highway, one may come on miners in desert and mountain areas. During the depression of the thirties, many jobless men from Los Angeles went out to San Gabriel Canyon, where there had been such a gold strike in the eighties that one saloon in which there was a dance every Saturday night—despite the fact that there was sawdust on the floor—found it profitable to pan out the sawdust every Sunday morning. Enough gold dust had been spilled to make it pay.

The prospectors who went there in the recent 'thirties declared they averaged three or four dollars' worth of gold a day. Major Sedley Peck, who was one of the organizers of American Legion Post No. 1 in Paris, has a little gold mine on his ranch in San Gabriel Canyon and declares that whenever he wants to he can work it and make fairly good wages. He works it only between casual jobs of writing but does well enough to attend all the Legion conventions and nearly always carries half a dozen little nuggets in his pocket. Only a few years ago, on Alder Creek, behind Mount Wilson and not far from Disappointment Peak, from which a person with good eyes can see the Los Angeles City Hall, a Captain Loomis, a retired Los Angeles policeman, homesteaded a place he had come on while hunting. He had a little gold mine on his place, from which he declared he was always able to dig from five to ten dollars' worth of gold in a day. And in the fringes of Sacramento one may still see gold buyers, equipped with gold scales, to whom the small-fry miners bring their gold to have it weighed and cashed in.

There still is gold in them thar hills and, all in all, there must be several thousand Californians who make the pursuit of it their life work. It's still an old California custom.

Many of the towns which produced millions during the Gold Rush and were scenes of boisterous activity are mere ghost towns today, and most of them have been plundered by souvenir hunters till little remains. The old town of Shasta, which is kept as a museum piece, is an exception. The first Masonic Hall in California, a solid brick building, still stands and is in use, and another building is a museum. A monument to the stage drivers who carried the gold out to Sacramento and San Francisco, in spite of hell and high water and Black Bart, stands out boldly on the one street. Almost all the buildings were of brick, and all were solid, with iron doors, for nearly every one of them held treasure in its time. Whether it was Wells Fargo office, saloon, or gaming house, each was a sort of bank, which would not only care for a miner's "dust" but defend it with guns and lives.

At least one historic mining town is to be preserved. That is Columbia, most of which has been acquired as a state park. In its heyday, the Fallon Theater there was almost as famous as Piper's Opera House in Virginia City, and Lola Montez, Lotta Crabtree, and many famous actors appeared there. That property now belongs to the College of the Pacific, the drama department of which will present the plays of Gold Rush days in it during the summers of 1948, 1949, and 1950, Columbia's centennial years. Persons who aided in the restoration of Williamsburg, Virginia, are interested in plans for restoring Columbia, which happily is so well preserved in the main it needs little restoration. They promise that as nearly as is possible—and lawful—in 1950 the Gold Rush will live again in Columbia.

IN CALIFORNIA'S pastoral days, the administration of law was a simple matter, largely based on friendship. The alcalde's silver-headed cane was the magic wand which set minds at ease and satisfied the demands of those whose feelings needed salve. Where a man could kill a steer if he was hungry or borrow a horse without consent, just so he gave some evidence he intended to return it, and where hospitality was so general an inn could not exist, there was little need for thievery, and where nearly all the white persons were related, there probably was a tendency to minimize other kinds of illegality. The presentation of the alcalde's cane, either by himself or by his messenger, was a summons to court. As late as 1845, Thomas Larkin wrote:

"In California there is a large allowance of laws sent in by the supreme government and as the paper is not very good to make paper seegars the law books are laid on the shelf. As the alcalde has neither sheriff nor constable, fees nor commission, and is forced to serve for one year, *nolens volens*, collecting debts is at the lowest stage. If a person with stolen property is brought forward and says he purchased the article from an Indian who has left for some other place, the trial may be put off till the Indian returns. Some people dislike prosecuting a man for stealing a horse for fear he will claim he was only bringing it back by a roundabout route and demand a dollar reward."

There had been a time when Governor Victoria boasted a man could leave his purse in the plaza at Monterey and find it when he returned, and he had a number of Indians shot for petty theft. But the Californians resented that as bloodthirsty. After all, they felt, the Indians were just behaving in a natural way, and Governor Victoria simply didn't understand them. He was an unpopular governor.

Yet banditry, or the law of force, was a time-honored institution. The Indians naturally had picked out the choicest places for their villages, and the first whites who came moved right in with them—and then moved the Indians out or generously allowed them to remain as servants. Sir Francis Drake, from the Spanish point of view, was nothing but a bandit seeking hiding places along the California Coast from which to surprise Manila galleons laden with riches. The ships' companies which came to trade with the Spanish settlers were all lawbreakers and practiced plenty of robbery in the form of trade. Since, prior to 1822, there were very few ships and no mercantile establishments of any kind in California, the settlers were at the mercy of the mariners for fifty-three years, as far as prices went. Hippolyte Bouchard, who landed and looted at will from Monterey to San Juan Capistrano, between which lie four hundred miles of coast, was a seafaring bandit.

But it took gold to turn banditry into an important industry in California and to develop some of America's most famous bandits.

Historian Bancroft seems to have had a soft spot in his heart for Joaquin Murrietta, the most dazzling of them all. He credits the story that Murrietta and his girl, Rosita, were mining and attending to their own business in the Stanislaus diggings when a group of American miners meaningly told Joaquin they wanted no "Greasers" there. Joaquin and Rosita moved to another place where some missionaries felt they were undesirables, probably because of the lack of the formality of marriage. Murrietta was only a boy of seventeen but he seems to have been a first-class monte dealer, so he entered a gambling house to make a living. A brother-in-law, arrested for another crime, said Murrietta had aided him in horse stealing. A posse hanged the brother-in-law. Murrietta fled and took a vow of vengeance.

His appeal was to the young Californians who felt the invading Americans were plundering the land. Within a few months he had a band which sometimes numbered as many as eighty, sometimes as few as twenty, but every man boasted he was a killer. From Shasta to Tulare they ravaged the land, and there is hardly a town in the Mother Lode country which does not have its legend of Joaquin.

In 1851, he attended a fandango in San Jose without being recognized and, when leaving, bowed over the hand of a dance partner and murmured: "Accept the compliments of Joaquin." Near Shasta, he so admired the pluck of a girl who had lassoed an elk that he rescued her from danger. In a gambling hall in Hangtown, when an American boasted he would kill Joaquin if he ever met him, a slender young man leaped on a table and announced that he was Joaquin. In 1852, he and his band drove three hundred stolen horses down into Sonora, Mexico, and such a drive of hundreds of miles must rank as a feat for a man for whom reward notices were posted everywhere and for whom all the sheriffs were looking. In Santa Barbara, a deputy sheriff named Wilson thought he had plans for capturing Murrietta, who was known to be in that vicinity. Every way out was guarded. Two Indians got into a fight in front of the hotel—hotels had come with the Gold Rush—in which Wilson was making headquarters, and when he stepped out to quell the trouble a bullet from somewhere else killed him. In 1853, Murrietta was recognized by two Americans who opened fire. He killed one, wounded the other, and escaped.

In May of that year, the legislature passed a special act authorizing Harry Love, a noted gun fighter, and twenty mounted rangers to hunt down Murrietta.

No doubt Murrietta's success was partly due to the fact that he was something of a hero to the rancheros. Certain it is that he was very attractive to the ladies. But one can't be attractive to too many ladies without losing the favor of earlier loves. Between 1851 and 1853, Rosita seems to have had several successors who began as lovers but became enemies. After the legislature passed that act, some of Joaquin's lieutenants proved traitors, too, and his current girl, Antonia de Molinari, rode away with one of them, Pancho Daniel.

Late in July, 1853, Love and eight rangers came on a group of six Mexicans in a pass. Apart from them was another Mexican, grooming a fine horse. Love began to question the other men when the man apart from them ordered: "I am in command here. Speak with me."

One of the rangers recognized the "commander" as Murrietta. Murrietta leaped on his horse, shouted to his followers to save themselves, and rode away. But the rangers were all good shots. The horse went down, and the rider died with three bullets through him. They took no chances with Joaquin Murrietta.

Murrietta had been only seventeen when he went from his native Sonora to the Mother Lode country in 1849. He was only twenty-one when he died. "In the canyons of California he was what Napoleon was in the cities of Europe, and displayed a high order of genius," Bancroft declares. "He regarded himself as a champion of his country rather than as an outlaw." And Bancroft seems to feel that some of the railroad and real-estate promoters of California did worse things to their fellow citizens than Murrietta did. However, Murrietta's band did terrible things. Manuel Garcia, one of his aides, known as Three-Fingered Jack because one finger had been shot off, had almost a passion for cutting Chinese throats, either for purposes of robbery or just for the fun of it. Many Chinese in the Mother Lode country washed out gold, and, as we have pointed out, the law did not permit an Indian or a Chinese to testify against a white man.

Love's rangers were so proud of what they had done that they cut off Murrietta's head and Three-Fingered Jack's mutilated hand for exhibition in San Francisco.

Vicente Chavez, another of Murrietta's lieutenants, was known as Fra Diablo. He was notable chiefly for an odd method of torture, sewing a man into a green bullhide, which tightened as it dried. According to accepted reports, Chavez was shot by accident.

Tibursio Vazquez came along a decade later but probably was inspired by Joaquin's example. He hailed from Monterrey, Mexico, and began murdering when he was fifteen years old. He made his headquarters in Los Angeles, and many a tourist has seen the Vazquez Rocks near that city. Indeed, almost all the world has seen them, for they have frequently been used as a "set" in motion pictures.

Some vast prehistoric cataclysm upended huge rocks, turning them into an ideal hideout for a robber band, one which any posse would approach with extreme caution, as it would have withstood any bomb of seventy-five years ago. Vazquez was half-Indian, cruel and brutish, and lacking the courtly graces of Murrietta, yet he was strangely attractive to the unpredictable sex.

He started early and worked hard at his criminal profession, yet no crime could be pinned on him till he was twenty-odd years old, and then all he was convicted of was horse stealing. He was released from San Quentin in 1863 and took up where he had left off. He flourished till 1874, when Sheriff Rowland of Los Angeles County trapped him in the cabin of a man known as Greek George. Tibursio leaped through a window, but someone in the posse wounded him, and he surrendered. No sooner was he put in jail in Los Angeles than maudlin women began showering sympathy on him. Nevertheless he was taken away to San Jose, a city in which those against whom prejudice ran high never have had a very good chance to escape. There he was tried for murder and hanged.

Vazquez was just a bad, bad boy, undeserving of the fame given him. His only notable achievement was the evasion of the law for well over a decade when most Californians carried guns and

the whole state was looking for him. As an individual he hardly seems as likable as Sanate, whose
promising career was cut short after only one
notable exploit. There was a ball in Los Angeles
to which Sanate was not invited. He and a few
friends attended unbidden, robbed the men, danced
with the women whether they would or not, ate
the supper, and departed with polite farewells. Apparently a confederate named Moreno killed
Sanate for the reward. When he brought in the
body to claim it he was a hero—till he was seen to
be wearing a watch stolen from one of the guests
at the ball and received a reward very different
from the one he had sought.

But the Mexicans didn't run away with all the
fame as bandits. Jack Powers, "Lord of the four
hundred gamblers of Angeles," had a picturesque
career. He participated in a war with the sheriff
of Santa Barbara County and won a few battles.
There was only one piece of artillery in Santa
Barbara, and Powers seized it and started march-
ing to his ranch. Sheriff Twiss pursued him but was
defeated with losses. Powers proceeded to his ranch
and fortified it, mounting stovepipe so it looked
like cannon. The sheriff was forced to raise the
siege. Powers and his gang did quite a bit of
plundering and murdering, and his name created
such dread that if anyone disappeared he was

feared to have fallen into the hands of Powers. There still are rumors of a hidden graveyard on the ranch.

Powers became southern California's champion outlaw in 1853, the last year of Murrietta's reign, but did not strain his luck too far. He is said to have died peaceably in Arizona without ever having paid for his crimes.

Tom Bell of Alabama, educated to be a doctor, seems to have outranked Powers as a human being if not as a violator of the law. Bell had six or eight followers in 1856, and they did their share of robbing. After robbing one victim who tried to flee and was shot, Bell bound up his wound to show his medical skill, though a wagon could be heard coming toward them. Bell held up the wagon, robbed the persons in it, made a bed for the wounded man in the bottom of it, and commanded the driver to be careful to avoid ruts in taking the wounded man to town. Bell was caught and executed in 1856.

California's star bandits, like its leaders in many other fields, were sometimes drawn from distant lands. Rattlesnake Dick was one whose past is obscure but who evidently wished his native land to get credit for his deeds. His short but notable career ended when a tax collector recognized him and led a sheriff to him. Dick killed the tax collector and wounded the sheriff, but the latter drilled him as he rode away. Next day Dick was found dead, with this note beside him: "Rattlesnake Dick dies but does not surrender, as do all true Britons."

When it came to literary expression, Black Bart was the standout among the Gold Rush bandits. Black Bart always worked alone, was always on foot, always carried a double-barreled shotgun, always held up stagecoaches driven by men who were accustomed to shooting it out with anyone who barred their way, always wore a flour sack over his head, and yet he flourished from 1875 to 1883. In that time he held up twenty-eight stagecoaches, always with the same words: "Throw down the box." Twenty-seven times the "box"— the Wells Fargo express box in which gold was being carried—was obediently thrown down to him. The twenty-eighth time it had been nailed to the floor, and that caused a delay which was Bart's undoing, even though he got the box.

The Mother Lode country is full of legends of Black Bart, many of them false. Joseph Henry Jackson, in *Tintypes in Gold*, has given all that can be proved of the character. But even that leaves one mystified by Bart's success. Posses scoured the countryside after every one of his robberies, but none overtook the lone man on foot. The crack detectives of the Wells Fargo Company laid traps for him which never worked. Tempting rewards hung over his head for years. He had no confederates or sympathizers who would lie for him, as Murrietta had. His voice, his walk, and his mannerisms were observed by many stagecoaches full of passengers. He left a sample of his handwriting the first time he robbed a stage. Yet when he was caught at last the persons closest to him were astonished, for they had always regarded him as a very proper gentleman.

Bart began his career with a declaration of war. After his first robbery he left this poetical effort for the detectives to pounce on:

"I've labored long and hard for bread,
  For honor and for riches,
But on my corns too long you've tread,
  You fine-haired sons of bitches."

Detectives and handwriting experts smiled happily and thought it wouldn't be long, but other successful robberies followed. The governor offered a reward, so did Wells Fargo, and the postal authorities added another. After the fourth robbery, skilled trackers were kept in readiness, and after the fifth robbery, they followed Bart's trail for sixty miles but lost it. From one woman and her sixteen-year-old daughter they got a description of a "traveling gentleman" who had stopped at their house and who, they were sure, was Bart. It was a pretty accurate description, too. The man's coat sleeve was ripped. His shoes had been cut with a knife, probably to make walking easier. His watch chain had been broken and repaired with leather. He had graying brown hair, thinning at the temples, and deep-set blue eyes. His hands were slender and genteel. "He looked like a preacher," said the woman.

Bart never killed anyone. Indeed, he never even hurt anyone. Once, when a frightened woman in a stagecoach he was robbing threw her purse to him, he tossed it back unopened. All he wanted was the Wells Fargo box and the mail. In his twenty-eight robberies he never fired a shot.

His success seems to have been due to strategy and surprise. From gossip in the towns he would learn when considerable amounts of gold were to be sent out. With only cheese and crackers he would camp out in the woods and carefully study the terrain, observing the time the stagecoaches passed certain points at which the driver and his armed guard, if he had one, would be most likely to have their attention centered on something ahead, or on the opposite side of the road. The lone bandit always had them covered with his shotgun before they knew he was near.

It was not the detectives, but a sixteen-year-old boy, who was Bart's undoing, though the detectives finished the job. The boy, Jimmy Rollerie, was going rabbit hunting. The stagecoach driver knew Jimmy, whose grandmother kept an inn, and gave him a lift. At the foot of a long grade Jimmy got off and started trudging through the brush.

The coach drove on. Just beyond the top of the grade Bart appeared with leveled shotgun.

The Wells Fargo Company had ordered the boxes nailed to the stage floor, so the driver couldn't throw down the box. Bart ordered the driver down, and the driver sensed a certain confusion and indecision.

"I can't get down," he said. "The brake's bad, and I have to hold it."

"It won't roll if you put a rock under the hind wheel."

"You do it then."

And Bart did it. He had the gun hand, he could have made someone else do it, but really he was a rather gentle robber. He pried the box loose, but it took time, and by that time Jimmy had come over the hill. He saw Bart backing out of the stage and realized he was seeing a hold-up.

As Bart made for the brush, Jimmy fired three shots. Bart got away but dropped a package which, when it was picked up, was found to be bloody. A handkerchief with a laundry mark on it was also found. Detectives located the laundry and found that the handkerchief had been sent to it by a Mr. Boulton.

When Bart finally was located he was found to be an elegantly dressed, dapper little man who wore a number six shoe and a derby hat and carried a cane. In his room was a Bible inscribed: "This Bible is presented to Charles E. Boles, 1st Sergeant, Co. B., 116th Ill. Inf., by his wife as a New Year's gift." He had taken the name of Black Bart from a story by a San Francisco lawyer. It was assumed he wore the derby hat under the flour sack he always wore over his head during robberies to give him the appearance of added height.

He was sentenced to San Quentin for seven years, but his conduct was perfect and he was released in 1888, though the San Francisco Examiner protested he had made some deal with the detectives for a light sentence in exchange for telling where some of his loot was. He was last definitely heard of in Japan, but in 1917 a New York newspaper carried a notice of the death of Charles E. Boles. If that Boles was Black Bart, he was eighty-seven years old.

Quite another form of banditry was that of the Americans who swept into California after the war with Mexico and stole the great estates of the Californians by semilegal means. They were aided by a Squatters Act and greatly encouraged by the Californians' utter lack of business methods. Notices in English were posted in post offices that Californians should present their proofs of owner- ship to their lands within a certain time, and those who did so satisfactorily were given United States patents to the land. But 1848 was nearly past when the first United States post office was opened in San Francisco. Few of the Californians could read Eng- lish, they did not frequent the few post offices which were established, and they did not dream that lands which had belonged to their families for generations could be taken from them because of failure to comply with legal technicalities of which they knew nothing. The metes and bounds of huge ranches had been fixed by landmarks which could easily be eradicated, such as blazed oak trees, or piles of stones on the edge of a creek with a Spanish name which had been supplanted by an American name.

In 1848, eight ranches near Los Angeles were in the hands of Americans who had married Cali- fornia girls, but in 1852 there were eighty ranches in that vicinity owned by Americans. In 1851, the *Los Angeles Star* protested "an act of Congress which should have been called an act to confiscate the private lands of the inhabitants of California," and in 1856 the pastors of the Episcopal, Methodist, Baptist, and Presbyterian churches in Los Angeles are said to have closed their church doors and left, abandoning the town as a den of iniquity.

Pio Pico, last Mexican governor of California, borrowed $80,000 and instead of a mortgage gave a deed to all his property, which a witness later testified was worth at least $750,000. When he realized his mistake, he tried to have the deed changed into a mortgage, but he lost everything and died in poverty in 1894, having been more or less sustained by his relatives for years.

The present cities of Oakland, Berkeley, and a few more were only part of the vast Peralta rancho. A man named Adams squatted on 160 acres of that land in 1850, driving stakes to mark out his claim to land everyone knew belonged to the Peraltas. The rancho had been granted to Don Luis Peralta in 1820 and consisted of 48,800 acres. Don Luis wished to divide it among his four sons, and when William Heath Davis had tried, in 1846, to buy the very land Adams pre-empted, Peralta had refused to sell. He needed it all for his sons and his great herds of cattle. But Adams not only helped himself and refused to move when ordered off, but went to San Francisco and got others to come across the bay and stake out claims beside his.

They slaughtered Peralta's cattle and did a thriving business of selling the meat to San Francisco butchers. Protected by the Squatters Act, Adams calmly went ahead and subdivided the land, selling lots to others, who also stole Peralta's cattle. At last the Peraltas went to law and finally got a judgment for a few thousand dollars, much less than they had spent in legal fees. But the land was never recovered.

That kind of banditry went on all over California. Even Americans who had married Californians were victimized by the element among the newcomers that was out for plunder. John Gilroy, for whom the town of Gilroy was named, was not an American but a Scot, who had married one of the Ortega girls. He was fleeced of his ranch of nine square miles. John Bidwell wrote: "Many old Californians made a distinction between the Gringo thieves and the manly pioneers who were good neighbors. A volume could be written about the unsolicited gifts of land—fifty acres here, one hundred acres there—made to Americans who had rendered the rancheros a service."

Even John Sutter, the great friend of every early American adventurer, in whose fort Frémont took refuge on March 9, 1846, and who had ended the Russian foothold in California by buying Fort Ross, could not call his vast domain his own when the gold seekers and squatters spread all over it. The gold found on his own land caused his impoverishment. The "kingdom" he had ruled so well and helped so much was swept from his grasp by a horde so numerous and overpowering it was like a devastating flood.

Such a lawless spirit had seized the land that on June 9, 1851, twenty men met in Sam Brannan's office in San Francisco to form the Vigilantes and draw up a constitution. "As neither life nor property is safe in San Francisco," the constitution declared, "the undersigned band themselves together in order to perform every lawful act to preserve the maintenance of law and order." Their first act was to arrest, try, and execute one of the "Sidney Ducks," or ex-convicts from Australia. For two months they patrolled the streets and met every ship from Australia to see that no more convicts were landed. You can get into plenty of arguments in San Francisco by either praising or denouncing the Vigilantes, and in an old churchyard there you can see tombstones which practically accuse them of murder, but when they disbanded, the ladies of Trinity Parish presented them with a banner and a testimonial of appreciation which read: "Do right and fear not."

In May, 1856, a summons went out calling "Members of the Vigilance Committee in good standing" to meet at 1005½ Sacramento Street that night at nine, "by order of the Committee of Thirteen." James King, who signed himself James King of William because there were numerous other James Kings, and who started the *San Francisco Bulletin*, had been shot to death by a man named James P. Casey. King had been a Vigilante in good standing. The committee led three thousand citizens to the jail and saved the county the bother of a trial in the case of Casey.

The Vigilantes were completely outside the law, and their executions were lynchings from the legal point of view. But they were proud of themselves, and most of their fellow citizens seem to have been proud of them. In 1857, they held a good-by parade with military bands. They marched in black frock coats buttoned to the throat like the Army uniforms of World War I, black pantaloons, white gloves, white satin badges, and cloth caps. The streets were decorated in their honor. Their officers were mounted. Some detachments carried muskets wreathed with flowers. Besides the horsemen, there were infantry and artillery in line. There were two squadrons of cavalry and a float with a replica of Fort Gunnysacks, said to have been their stronghold.

Can you imagine anything like that in any important American city other than San Francisco?

Mere mention of Vigilantes suggests San Francisco, yet the first Vigilance Committee had been organized in Los Angeles in 1836, fifteen years before one was formed in San Francisco. Today Los Feliz Boulevard is an important street in Los Angeles, and many persons with a smattering of Spanish smile at such a name for a street, as *"los feliz"* means "the happy." But it was not named for those who live there now, nor was the old gentleman for whom it was named happy. His name was Domingo Los Feliz, and the present boulevard more or less follows the old road which led to Rancho Los Feliz. Maria del Rosario Villa was young and vivacious. Domingo was passé, but he was wealthy. There was pomp when he married Maria, but there was a false note in the rejoicing. She was a tantalizing vixen, who kept poor Domingo straining after happiness that was just beyond his reach. Then a vaquero from Sonora, whose dash and daring fascinated Maria, drifted into San Gabriel. Maria left her husband to elope with the vaquero. She was much too noticeable a person to keep hidden and soon was found, but petulantly refused to leave a lover for a mere husband.

Domingo's Spanish pride was in the dust, but he still loved the girl. Apparently the law, as administered in California then, could do nothing for him, so he appealed to the Church. The long arm of the Church reached out, and Maria consented to return to Rancho Los Feliz. But Domingo had to go after her.

They started home, riding on one horse as was the custom because so many horses needed the strong hand of a man. Domingo was demonstrating that he still could hold his own on a horse. But in a lonely place in the trail, Alipas, the vaquero, appeared like a bandit and stabbed Domingo in the back. Then Alipas and Domingo's loving wife dragged the body into the brush, covered it with leaves, and left together. Five days later the body was found. Alipas and the woman were discovered in San Gabriel, and the law asserted itself. They were arrested and brought to Los Angeles. Domingo Los Feliz had been an esteemed citizen, and indignation seethed. If a stranger from Mexico could come in and defy the laws of church and custom that way, there was no safety for anyone. So fifty of the town's most prominent men, according to J. Gregg Layne, editor of the *Quarterly of the Historical Society of Southern California*, met at the home of Don Juan Temple a week later and decided that as no punishment had yet been meted out it was time to act.

At two o'clock that afternoon the committee demanded the prisoners. The jailer refused to hand over the keys but submitted quietly when they were taken from him. The two culprits were hanged, their bodies were exposed in front of the jail as a warning for two hours, and then, "after offering their services to the alcalde to aid in preserving law and order, the committee of fifty of the best citizens of Los Angeles quietly dissolved."

Such mingling of snap-judgment justice, impulsive lawlessness, and judicial dignity was typical of California's evolutionary days, and to some extent still is today. There are still two or three counties in which the administration of law often makes persons in other counties blink, and it is not unusual for the state's attorney general to have to step into a trial which is purely a county matter because local prejudices and antagonisms are so high there is danger Justice will be blind in only one eye but winking with the other. For that, to a considerable extent, is an old California custom.

I T'S a California custom, old, new, and in the middle, to speak in superlatives. Californians love to point to something of theirs as the oldest, biggest, richest, most famous, or most wonderful "in the world." Henry Watterson once was quoted —and maybe he was quoting—as saying: "In California every bush is a tree, every hill a mountain, and every man a damned liar."

Unquestionably we Californians are unconscious

[157]

liars part of the time, for we get so in the habit of thinking that if it's Californian it must be the greatest of its kind, that we don't go to the bother of checking up on the rest of the world to see if possibly we are wrong.

Mother Nature is partly responsible. She put Mount Whitney, which reaches an altitude of 14,496 feet, and Death Valley, 279 feet below sea level, in the same California county, and they are only eighty miles apart. They are the highest and lowest points in the United States, and Death Valley is one of the two lowest spots in the world. The giant sequoias are the hugest trees "in the world" and probably the oldest living things—the age of the General Sherman in Sequoia National Park is estimated by scientists at 4,500 years. It is 108 feet in circumference one foot above the ground, as measured by John Muir. A thousand tourists daily are assured that the Founders Tree on the Redwood Highway, towering to a height of 364 feet, is the tallest in the world—though the encyclopedia says that Australian blue gums reach more than 400 feet. The Golden Gate landlocks one of the most magnificent harbors in the world. In addition to precious metals, California's mineral wealth includes vast quantities of oil, and in agriculture California leads the world. In 1946, the agricultural products of Los Angeles County totaled $214,820,957, topping all other counties in the United States. The next three counties were all in California, as were eleven of the twenty leading counties. The biggest vineyard, the biggest hay market, the biggest fruit orchard all are claimed by California. Lake Tahoe, the surface of which is 6,225 feet above sea level, is one of the highest big lakes "in the world" and is more than 1,600 feet deep. Ribbon Fall in Yosemite, which tumbles down 1,612 feet, is the tallest "in the world." San Francisco had a bitter fight in 1947 because Mayor Lapham wished to do away with the cable-car lines, for A. S. Hallidie of San Francisco had invented the cable-car idea to overcome San Francisco's hills, and he and William Eppelsheimer had built the first cable-car line "in the world" in 1873. Southern Californians say George Chaffey first proved that hydroelectric energy could be conducted long distances.

Man has tried to compete with nature in creating wonders. Near Sacramento today you may see boats bigger than those which sailed around the Horn to discover California, floating in lakes which weren't there last year and won't be there next year. Those boats are owned by companies which can put hundreds of thousands of dollars into equipment. They are hydraulic mining outfits, filled with powerful machinery. A year ago, the lakes in which they float may have been lovely fruit orchards which the mining companies have bought up and from which they have shorn the trees. Water has been piped in to form the lakes and float the dredges. After yielding gold for a hundred years, California is still the greatest gold-producing state in the Union. In 1946 it produced $12,184,000 worth.

Hoover Dam isn't in California, but it was built for California, to which most of its water and its electric energy go. It rises 726 feet and turns the Colorado River into a lake well over 100 miles long. The Golden Gate Bridge and the Bay Bridge connecting San Francisco and Oakland are champions in their classes. The Central Valley project, when it is completed, will fairly make nature groggy, changing it from an irresistible force into the slave of man. Shasta Lake, covering 6,815 square miles, is the greatest man-made lake lying wholly within one state, and, with snowcapped Mount Shasta for its background and great forests all around, is one of the most beautiful. Having no natural harbor, Los Angeles has built what it calls "the greatest man-made harbor in the world," and with 453 square miles in its city limits Los Angeles surely is one of the world's biggest cities in area. It also unblushingly claims to be the world capital for motion pictures, radio, aviation, and sportswear.

To Speak in Superlatives

It asserts that more "famous" writers, actors, stage and costume designers, and musicians live there than anywhere else "in the world." It is sure Hollywood Bowl is the greatest amphitheater for symphony concerts. The University of California, though not founded till 1868, is the greatest state university. With its branches, it has about 45,000 full-time students. In Santa Rosa you are shown the home of Luther Burbank and assured he was the "greatest" inspirer of agricultural progress.

Perhaps Californians brag about the weather in superlatives more often than they do anything else. When they get far from home they tell how they can eat Christmas dinner outdoors and bask in sunshine in January. They fail to add that in Los Angeles it isn't safe to turn off the furnace heat before July, unless one has a good fire laid in the grate to light up in case company comes in.

The dwellers in the Mojave Desert write friends in Los Angeles: "We're planning to bring a bus load of high-school kids to Los Angeles to see a fog. They've heard guests at dude ranches speak of fogs so often they think they'd like to see one for themselves." Persons living within forty miles of the sea retort by telling the story of the stranger in the desert who asked: "Does it ever rain here?" to which the desert rat replied: "Sure, it does. I've never seen it myself, but my grandfather saw it once." It is a fact that some parts of the desert may get only a trace of rain in a whole year, but it is also a fact that there's usually enough moisture to bring out the desert wildflowers in the early spring.

A guest ranch near Victorville advertises it will not charge guests for any day when the sun does not shine, but the desert is full of surprises. Once I took my family for a week end to Palm Springs, where winter sunshine would make swimming in the hotel pool a pleasure. That night the weather changed so surprisingly we had to use extra blankets. Early in the morning my three-year-old son, who had never seen snow, came toddling into the room my wife and I occupied calling: "Look out the window, Mommy. It's rainin' cotton!" By breakfast time there were four inches of snow on the level patio, and the children had a wonderful time making snowmen. The Indian chief in the near-by reservation said it was the first snow in eighty-nine years, but brief, heavy showers are likely to occur at any time.

When James Rolph was governor he urged that Californians wear straw hats the year around to advertise their climate. The joke of that brag was that the governor was a San Franciscan, and the average San Franciscan never wears a straw hat. Stroll up Market Street on an August day for several blocks and you will see no straw on the natives. If you are wearing one you may be asked: "How are things down in L.A.?"

Similarly, the average southern California man who buys a business suit in August expects to wear it right on through the summer and fall and winter and spring, as long as it lasts. In summer he leaves off the vest and in winter often needs not only the the vest but a top coat, but nine-tenths of the men's suits sold are for all-year wear. Most men buy slacks and sport coats, too, but they also are for all-year wear.

It is doubtful if there is any part of southern California which does not boast that its climate is "the finest in the world." Between Capistrano and San Diego there is so little difference between winter and summer temperatures that perhaps one hundred thousand average families along the coast have no heat in their homes except what comes from the gas stove in the kitchen and, if their houses or apartments are so situated their coolers can catch the sea breeze, require no refrigerators in summer, though they usually try to use up meats and milk within twenty-four hours of their delivery.

From 50 to 150 miles east of the coast, sometimes in those same countries, the summer heat might be anywhere from 100 to 130 degrees, but the date-rancher beside Salton Sea will assure you as earnestly and honestly that his climate is "the best in the world" as does the realtor in San Diego within sight of the blue and silver sea. He will tell you how he or one of his children was looking death in the eyes when they moved to the desert, "but now he feels like a million dollars." One man in El Centro who had a light truck and did odd jobs of hauling was asked if he could make a living that way. He solemnly answered: "My business is worth five hundred dollars a week to me . . . I take in about thirty dollars a week and the way I feel out here is worth the other four-seventy."

In other words, it's an old California custom to brag about what you've got, even if it's something that makes persons from elsewhere shrink in fear, and to "sell" it to them if possible. And every California community is full of Exhibit A's.

In 1906, Jimmy Swinnerton, originator of the comic strip and famous painter of desert scenes, was told by a New York doctor that he had only a month to live. On the way to the desert he met another man who was pacing nervously up and down the coach, wringing his hands at intervals. Finally Jimmy asked:

"Friend, is there something weighing on your mind?"

The other fixed him with a stare like that of the Ancient Mariner and croaked:

"I've got only a month to live!"

"That's remarkable," said Jimmy, with bright interest. "I'm in exactly the same fix. What date do you die?"

The other stared a moment, then burst into a laugh.

Forty years later, a stalwart character apparently good for another twenty years, Swinnerton was at the peak of his career and making a great success of his fifth marriage. His humor, philosophy, and common-sense way of living may have been mainly responsible for his recovery, but a dozen California and Nevada desert towns boast that their climate did it all.

San Franciscans proudly tell you theirs is the greatest show town "in the world." That claim takes us back to Gold Rush days. There is a legend that, when saloons had stages and gave their patrons the only theatrical entertainment, there were two, side by side, named La Bella and The Union. A ship arrived from Lima, Peru, and its officers rather loftily told the San Franciscans that in Lima they had a grand-opera troupe from Europe. The miners didn't care a hoot for grand opera, but if that was what the swells thought was tony they weren't going to let any town in South America look down on them. San Francisco must have the best, no matter what it cost and whether they liked it or not.

They planked down gold dust on the bar till there was enough money to bring the opera troupe to San Francisco. But when it arrived no stage in San Francisco could accommodate it. So the partition between La Bella and The Union was knocked out, their two stages were made into one, and thereafter the rival concerns proceeded as one, the famous Bella Union.

There's a wide range between Lotta Crabtree and grand opera, but San Francisco loved and still loves them both. When, as a child, Lotta began dancing and singing in the mining camps, the miners flung pokes of gold dust and nuggets at her feet, and later San Francisco made her such an idol that when she died she left an estate of nearly four million dollars, most of which went to veterans of World War I. She built the city a fountain in what then was the heart of the theatrical district, and Tetrazzini sang on the steps of that fountain as a testimonial to Lotta.

San Franciscans bid five hundred dollars a seat for the opening performance of Edwin Forrest in Shakespearean drama. They presented Adelina Patti with a diamond sunburst and Sarah Bernhardt with a laurel wreath. In 1931, the news that an old actor, unknown to fame, was dying in poverty made San Franciscans chip in to a fund to have him taken to the best hospital and given the best of care as long as he lived. And many an actor who rose to high standing was given his real start by a benefit performance which sent him away to New York with pockets bulging.

The Magnificent Ralston built a theater to house a stock company headed by Lawrence Barrett and John McCullough, and Bret Harte wrote an ode for its opening. Modjeska's first performance in English was given in San Francisco and launched her on her great career. John Drew the elder and Joseph Jefferson made their starts there in burlesque. William A. Brady, David Belasco, David Warfield, Maude Adams all got their starts there, Belasco and Warfield as ushers in the Bush Street Theater. A German beer hall named the Tivoli pirated a production of "Pinafore" and grew into the only home of an operatic stock company, which performed seven days a week for forty years. It was the training school, according to Charles Caldwell Dobie's *San Francisco,** for many great stars. The great Luisa Tetrazzini made her American debut there at a top price of fifty cents. The tenor sang in English, the baritone in Italian, the soprano in German, but it was all one to San Francisco, if they sang well.

Nance O'Neil, Maxine Elliott, Holbrook Blyn, Edna Wallace Hopper, Florence Roberts, Alice Neilsen, and Isadora Duncan were others who owed

* Quotations from the book by permission of Appleton-Century Co.

their starts to San Francisco. "When I first saw Isadora Duncan," writes Dobie, "she was teaching reluctant boys the polka." He was one of the reluctant boys. Maude Allen was another dancer who got her start there, and later she was a sensation in London as *Salome*. Sybil Sanderson started there and rose to such international fame that it was for her Massenet wrote *Thaïs*.

When it is realized that many of those "greats" were started confidently on their way before San Francisco had three hundred thousand inhabitants, it is pretty hard to contest the boastful claims of San Franciscans. Certainly they have set an example to most of America, outside New York, in appreciating their own and helping them get ahead. Even when Los Angeles had grown to twice the size of San Francisco, it still had to get its grand opera from San Francisco, which through the years has maintained a splendid organization. In 1932, San Francisco dedicated its handsome War Memorial Opera House, seating three thousand five hundred, which is crowded for practically every performance.

Transportation and speed always have intrigued Californians. They will tell you that Paul Revere was all right, but John Brown, not of Kansas but of California, did a greater thing. As night closed in on September 23, 1846, the American garrison left to hold Los Angeles was in a serious situation. It couldn't hold out long, and the army which had marched on to the north must be informed. Brown, known as "Juan Flaco" or "Long John," could speak Spanish and could ride. At eight P.M. he dashed past the besieging lines of Californians, before they realized he was not one of their own, and was on his way. He arrived in San Francisco on September 28, just four days later to the hour, after riding 630 miles, believed to be an all-time record for one rider.

Californians also claim credit for the first coast-to-coast automobile trip, the first transocean plane trip—for Lindbergh prepared at and started from San Diego—and so many other firsts that if we don't watch ourselves we're likely to be claiming Adam. Among other blessings to humanity, we claim that the white line for highways was the invention of a Redlands man. Then there is the boast of Los Angeles that it possesses the world's shortest railway, Angels Flight, which is only 325 feet long. In Santa Maria they like to tell you they have the widest streets platted in any original townsite, all planned so six-horse teams could be swung in them.

Some of California's superlatives are a little too exaggerated to hold water, like that of Walter Colton who, in 1844, declared that "in the humblest hovel in California there is more joy than in princely palaces," or the assertion of José de Jesus Vallejo, in 1842, that the soldiers of Governor Micheltoreno were such a pack of cowards "that our rancheros, mounted on their horses and carrying in their arms their young children, fought one against three and vanquished them."

When they counted the palms in Thousand Palms Canyon in the Borrego Valley they found that by count there were only 258. In Lassen National Park they quite proudly assure you that Mount Lassen is the only active volcano in the United States. In 1915, it put on a full scale eruption and, like many of us, it can't seem to quit smoking, though apparently it has been trying to swear off ever since. It must be confessed that we Californians find it even harder to swear off speaking in superlatives, though it must also be confessed few of us seem to try very hard. And, after all, why should we?

FEELING at home in the out of doors is one
of the oldest of California customs. The early settlers had to do it, as they were only campers at first,
and their homes began as one-room adobe huts.
Most of the time they cooked outdoors, ate outdoors,
did all their entertaining outdoors, and were as
accustomed to sleeping outdoors as to sleeping
indoors. Because of the absence of markets or
stores, the shopper for meat went outdoors to kill

a bear, an elk, or an antelope, or to rope a bullock and cut off a few steaks or roasts for dinner. The housewife went shopping in the woods, the only place to find berries, nuts, greens, water cress, and wild onions and garlic, and, as honey often was the only sugar obtainable for months or even years, she kept an alert pair of eyes on the lookout for bee trees.

The houses grew, but the families grew faster, as marriage ties linked households together. Still there were no inns for a people probably more addicted to parties and to visits than any other people ever were. Few persons between the ages of six and seventy-five hesitated when asked to rid horseback a hundred miles to attend a party, and when they got there all the men expected to use their saddles for pillows, their serapes for blankets, and pine needles, straw, or plain sod for a mattress.

The twenty-one missions in the chain were about thirty miles apart, which was supposed to be an average day's walk for a Franciscan friar. Father Serra, first president of the missions, arrived at San Diego by ship and went from there to Monterey by ship, but he is believed to have walked from Mexico City to the west coast and is said to have walked the length of the chain of California missions five times. He took ship at Monterey in order to return to Mexico City to have Governor Fages removed from office, but returned after that was accomplished and is supposed to have walked all the way while in Mexico, as the Franciscans were not supposed to ride. On one occasion he was asked to ride in a palanquin but refused, saying the horse needed the rest more than he did.

But early Californians who were not friars spent most of their lives on horseback. One writer declares that as soon as a baby was born and dressed it was given to a man on horseback, who rode posthaste with it to the nearest mission, accompanied by a large party of the infant's relatives and its godparents, who had been picked out months before. "From that time, hardly a day passed, from the cradle to the grave, when the newcomer was not on horseback."

With crowds far bigger than any house could hold, most of the amusements were out of doors, too. The gathering of berries was an essential part of the year's work in the sugarless era, but every community made a picnic of it. We have already seen that the rodeo was a California invention. In 1770, a decree was issued requiring all owners of cattle to have registered brands, and the annual rodeo, or roundup, had the backing of law. The alcalde would call the people of a community together by having a drum beaten, and would announce that the rodeo would be at a certain time and place. Everyone interested had to be present, and everyone else went along for the fun. Whole families went, and, of course, most of them had to camp. It was business, for there was an official *juez de campo*, or judge of the field, whose word was law if there was any dispute over the ownership of calves or cattle, but there was so much feasting and dancing and sport it was business from which no one wished a vacation, or even an hour off.

Vaqueros trained for such events as earnestly as football teams train for a Rose Bowl game today, and the adherents of every rancho were on hand to cheer their champions. Even on the military reservations there were rodeos, for the soldiers had to raise their own meat or obtain it by hunting. The missions also had them. There were five thousand Indians at San Jose, for example, and every Saturday one hundred cattle were killed to provide for them.

At every mission there was a *calaveras*, or place of skulls, where the bones and unused parts of the slaughtered animals were thrown, usually in sequestered ravines, and those places attracted so many bears that young bloods who wished to lasso bears and drag them through the villages always knew where to go. North of San Francisco bears were so numerous that Señora Vallejo said she had seen them in the courtyard of her house, and

women as well as men there carried rifles and
pistols. One of the early Spanish governors directed
an official bear hunt in the San Luis Obispo area for
the purpose of laying in a large supply of meat, and
later another governor appointed an official bear
hunter, "to trap in pits, shoot or lasso bears." José
Ramon Carrillo went bear-hunting armed only
with his *reata* and a knife. After roping the bear he
would dismount and advance on foot, holding a
bullhide shield. When the grizzly lunged for him,
he parried with the shield and killed with the knife.

There were no bathing beauty contests in those
days, but Mrs. de Packman reports that in *California de antes* it was the custom for the virgins to
bathe out of doors on San Juan's day, going to a
secluded, willow-screened place near Los Angeles,
where a dam created a pretty good swimming pool.
But after American settlers came in, one of them
got hold of land adjoining that dam—and also, it
is suspected, learned of the custom—for he also
used the willows as a screen and, at what seemed
a propitious moment, when the girls were far from
their clothes, mischievously opened the flood gate
of the dam, so that suddenly the embarrassed
young women found themselves in very shallow
water.

G. M. Guinn, writing of Los Angeles in about
1830, said: "The houses were built for utility rather

than beauty. The people made the outdoors their real home." Alvarado is authority for the statement that José Castro, on occasions, was in the saddle thirty-six hours at a stretch, speaking of it as if it were something of a habit. A man like that hardly needed a house to live in. But perhaps nothing indicates better what hardy outdoor people the early settlers of California were than the fact that De Anza's party of 240 colonists, which marched overland from San Miguel de Horcasitas, Sonora, Mexico, to found San Francisco on September 17, 1776, made the trip with the loss of only one member by death, whereas eight persons were born en route. One of them, Salvador Ignacio Linares, was the first white child born in California. He was born at Warner's Hot Springs on Christmas Eve, 1775, but apparently the caravan halted only long enough for a celebration, for it reached San Gabriel January 4, 1776.

In that trek over trackless deserts and mountains which towered as high as eleven thousand feet, De Anza's party marched more than a thousand miles through some of the most hostile country nature has created. Man has made much of it inviting now, but then the desert was heartbreakingly desolate, the mountains heartbreakingly forbidding in winter.

Heredity and opportunity have combined to make

Californians carry on their tradition of outdoor living. Close to fifty million acres of California are still open to the public, in state or national parks or desert or mountain areas which never have been homesteaded. Most of the land still available for homesteading is so arid or so inaccessible that only a very hardy hermit could live on it, and if he had a wife she probably wouldn't live there with him, but it is all inviting to the person who wishes to pack in where the mountain fishing is good, or go to the desert to sleep in a sleeping bag where the stars hang low and loom large. Probably more sleeping bags are owned in California than in any other state.

But it is in the average home that outdoor living comes within the reach of all. The Spanish settlers built their homes around a patio in which there were flowers and grass and maybe a fountain, and present-day Californians have adopted the patio idea. They do not build fortress-houses around it, as the early Californians did, but they still love to have barbecue fireplaces and eat outdoors and spend a great deal of time outdoors. The girls want places where they can lie on the grass in sunsuits and cultivate tan; the boys think if the family hasn't a swimming pool it isn't keeping up with the Joneses. The back-yard swimming pool was a California idea, and in southern California there are thousands of them, fully half of them in the yards of persons who could get in their cars and be at the seashore in ten minutes. If you go to call on a movie star you are likely to find him or her sitting in the patio in a bathing suit, and occasionally diving into the swimming pool for a brisk swim. "If I swim up and down that pool about twenty times every day," one of them says, "I can keep my figure right, without starving. If I don't, I put on weight."

Drive-ins are another California invention. Drive-in restaurants became so popular in southern California that drive-in theaters—in which one can sit in one's car and see the show—drive-in markets, and even drive-in banks have made their appearance. They say Lucky Baldwin was the cause of the first drive-in bank. He didn't like to leave his spirited horses, or bother to hitch them to a hitching post, so he would merely drive up in front of the bank and blow a horn, and a bank clerk would run out to wait on him.

Incidentally, the filling station was a California invention, and the first of its widely popular drive-ins. Many readers can remember when the corner grocery was the place at which motorists got their gasoline. Earl C. Anthony of Los Angeles, one of that city's first automobile dealers, was traveling in France, when he came on a Frenchman who had rigged up a hose to convey petrol into motor cars, instead of using a funnel to pour it from cans, as was the general practice. Anthony returned to Los Angeles and proposed to Don Lee, another motor-car dealer, that they get engineers to improve on the Frenchman's idea. They did so, with the co-operation of still another dealer, and opened the world's first filling station. But no customers came, so they resorted to trickery, or business strategy, if you prefer. Each of them had many motor vehicles in his show rooms, so they hired drivers for them and had them line up at a busy time of day, as if waiting in line to get into the filling station. They had enough in line to create a traffic congestion and start everyone talking about their new venture.

Those who talked loudest were the grocers, who resented having what promised to become important business taken from them. They declared it was dangerous to have more than fifty gallons of gasoline in any one place within the city limits and demanded an ordinance to forbid it. That forced the filling-station operators to go underground—bury their storage tanks and take other measures to prevent fire and explosion hazards. But they met all safety requirements and won.

Sunbathing is such a California custom that one Los Angeles manufacturer put out a sun tent, with sides but no roof, which could be set up on the roofs of apartment houses and other buildings. It looked as if he had struck a gold mine, till, at the beginning of the late war, aviation filled the southern California sky with fliers, many of whom flew low because of the sunbathers. Blimps also added to their embarrassment, and then the shortage of canvas, because so much was needed for Army and Navy purposes, put an end to the business temporarily.

Visitors get infected with the sunbathing craze, too, not because they are so eager for a coat of tan, but because they think it is good for them. When Dr. Einstein visited at Palm Springs, a young woman reporter called at the home at which he was visiting but was told she couldn't see the great scientist. Baffled but not beaten, she pretended to be leaving but hid in the garden and flitted from bush to bush to see if she couldn't find Dr. Einstein there. She did, but did not interview him. The Doctor was stretched on a couch getting full benefit of the desert sun on his bare skin.

In many states, only the well-to-do have vacation cottages of any kind. In California, tens of thousands of school teachers, mechanics, carpenters, truck drivers, and newspaper reporters, among others, own some beach, mountain, or desert "shack" which usually is more than a shack. It is a place to which one can get away for a week-end and enjoy an entire change of scene and activity.

Carl B. Glasscock, whose books on western historical epochs form a fascinating library in themselves, came nearer to having the world by the tail than most writers. When he quit newspaper work to make a career of book writing, he owned a charming but modest home in a beach resort. At that time, such a place would rent for only about fifty dollars a month in winter but for four or five times that much in summer. From November to June, he would make a systematic job of research, getting all his notes in order. Then he would rent his house, and he and his wife would go to Sequoia National Park, Yosemite, or some other place where they could rent a mountain cabin and be far from interruption, and he would write his book. Every book was such a thorough job it made its readers wish to read more of Glasscock's books, and when his fourteenth book came out his first was still selling well. For twenty years he found great enjoyment in both his daily work and his daily living, with freedom from tension, strain, and worry, and with growing prosperity. It was as near perfection as one can get in this imperfect world. But life is a quirky thing. A man living so wisely should have lived to a great age, but Carl died in middle age.

Glasscock is mentioned only as an illustration. Many thousands of Californians manage to order their lives and their business so as to spend certain

seasons in the out-of-doors. Those who have beach
or mountain cabins not only go to them but invite
many friends. All the state and national parks have
camp grounds, trailer camps, cabins, or tent cottages, and those few Californians who do not pos-
sess motor cars can get to most of those places by
bus. A state with a thousand miles of ocean front
has plenty of beach, and even in midwinter many
persons go to the beaches in southern California.
Many habitually get themselves photographed in
the surf every New Year's Day so they can send the
pictures to eastern relatives. Confidentially, I have
done that myself, and unless one is hardened to it
by daily surf-bathing, the water and the air seem
doggoned cold. However, there are many persons
who vow they enjoy it, and when a twenty-five-
thousand-dollar prize was offered to the winner of a
New Year's swim from Los Angeles harbor to Catalina Island, a distance of about twenty-six miles,
there were scores of contestants. One woman living
in one of the beach towns boasted for years that
she had never missed a day of surf bathing up to
her sixty-fifth year.

In winter, many of those same southern Californians go in for snow sports as enthusiastically as
do people in northern climates. With peaks ranging
from seven thousand to eleven thousand feet within
easy reach, skiing and tobogganing are popular,

and one of the West's best outfitting places for skiers is in Los Angeles. At some of those winter-sports festivals one may see girls in bathing suits on skis, the argument being that the bright sunshine makes such apparel quite in order. It is one of southern California's advertising stunts, however, and the girls get pretty cold sometimes, as do those similarly attired who appear in Pasadena's Tournament of Roses parade on New Year's Day.

But it all goes back to tradition. The man who introduced snow sports in California was Snowshoe Thompson, a hero of the Gold Rush days. In 1856, Thompson, a Scandinavian, lived just inside the California line near Lake Tahoe. He carried the mail to the scattered mining camps and, when snows came which piled up twenty feet deep in the mountain passes, he made himself a pair of snowshoes, the first ever seen in California, so that the miners might get their mail.

For twenty-six years Thompson delivered the mail on snowshoes throughout the winter. From Carson City, Nevada, to Placerville, California, a distance of a hundred miles, he maintained the tradition that the mail must go through. Over Donner Pass, where the Donner Party was snowed in and thirty-nine of its eighty-seven members died in one of the West's historic tragedies in 1846, Thompson skimmed his lonely way, that other lonely men

[183]

might get letters from home. There were times when deep snows put the Pony Express out of commission, and when hostile Indians made most men afraid to move about except in strong and well-armed groups. But nothing stopped Snowshoe Thompson and his homemade snowshoes. When blizzards drove every other living creature to shelter, he sailed out of them like Thor, with his beard frozen stiff and his cap and clothes coated with ice.

It is not recorded that Thompson was rewarded with any notable amount of worldly goods. But his name and fame have become a legend, and his simple devotion to duty an inspiration. And that legend has made all California, even that part of it which basks in a midwinter climate suitable for palms and roses, aware that it is snow country.

THE telling of tall tales for the hoaxing of
tenderfeet and tourists is an old California custom
which has added much to the mirth of nations—
often to the great embarrassment of innocent and
credulous victims. One tall tale, the story of the
Jumping Frog of Calaveras County, made Mark
Twain famous, and only a few were cruel or
vicious in intent. But the Gold Rush miners felt the
same right to haze newcomers that college boys do

today, and did it for somewhat the same purpose—
the testing of their qualities of sportsmanship and
intelligence. They vied with one another in the
telling of incredible yarns with poker faces, and
Mark Twain was only falling in with the custom
of the time and place when he began to write stories
of imaginary events as if he were reporting actual
happenings.

Before the Americans came, the Spaniards told
tall tales of their own, but they were all offered as
truth and were mostly of deeds of chivalry and
prowess. A sample is the story of a horseman at San
Jose, who won a wager that he could ride his horse
at full speed while carrying a salver holding a
dozen wine-glasses, filled to the brim, and after
riding fifty rods could stop suddenly and hand
down the salver without a drop having been
spilled. The polite Spaniards accepted that as truth,
just as today many of us accept flattering legends
about our favorite politicians. But many of the Gold
Rush miners were from Missouri and had to be
shown. They were contemptuous of what they
thought was the Spaniards' childlike gullibility,
and spun tall tales of their own for the amusement
of those who were gifted with "savvy" and the
embarrassment of those who weren't.

In that atmosphere Mark Twain quickly made
himself at home. In that vein he reported the dis-

covery of a petrified man in the Washoe district. The *San Francisco Bulletin* of October 15, 1862, carried the story thus:

"The body was in a sitting position, leaning against a huge mass of outcroppings. The attitude was pensive, the right thumb resting against the side of the nose. The left thumb partially supported the chin, the forefinger pressing the lower corner of the left eye and drawing it partly open. The right eye was closed and the fingers of the right hand spread apart. The verdict of the jury was that the victim came to his death by protracted exposure." Just rest your right thumb against the side of your nose and spread the fingers apart to get part of the picture.

In similar vein, Mark wrote a society item about a ball given in honor of his having paid his board bill, with descriptions of costumes and everything. He reported his own costume thus: "Mr. Lawlor's shirt, Mr. Ridgeway's vest, Mr. Wagner's coat, Mr. Camp's hat, Mr. Peyton's boots, Jerry Long's white kids, Judge Gilchrist's cravat, the Unreliable's brass seal ring and Dr. McDonald's pantaloons."

Mark's lack of worldly goods was the source of much of his humor in that period. Once a friend met him standing on a street corner in San Francisco as if undecided what to do and holding a cigar box under one arm.

"What are you doing?" asked the friend. Mark looked down at the cigar box.

"Oh, I'm moving again," he said.

The story of the jumping frog, according to Ivan Benson's *Mark Twain's Western Years*, was an old one at Jackass Hill. Many a raconteur had tried his tongue at it, but none had put it on paper. And, of course, none ever told it as Sam Clemens did. That piece of humor swept across the country and won Clemens his first national recognition, proving that the rest of the country liked tall tales as much as the miners did. Now the annual jumping-frog contest is held at Angels Camp and attracts not only frogs from as far away as Arkansas and Louisiana and Florida but such a horde of visitors the highways of the Mother Lode country are as crowded with traffic as are city streets.

A later form of hoaxing the stranger, especially the city slicker, was the Casey Run, invented at Benicia. In the early days, eager promoters declared that San Francisco was no place for a town and that Benicia would be the great city on San Francisco Bay. They tooted its horn so loudly they got the state capital located there and built the first capitol building, a brick structure now used as the Benicia Public Library. But a little less than a year later the legislature changed its mind and chose Sacramento as the capital.

The loss of the capital burst Benicia's boom, and it became a very dull place. However, in the early days all the transportation that wasn't by horseback was by ship or steamboat, and Benicia was a place at which people waited—and waited and waited, sometimes—for transportation either upriver or downbay, and those who craved excitement complained of its dullness.

Benicians resented such criticism and, when it came from anyone who sneered at their town, they were eager to punish him, if he looked young or vain enough to be susceptible. They artfully told him about the beautiful Casey girls, who dearly loved a good time but whose father was a fierce and dangerous person. He kept those poor, fun-loving girls shut up like nuns on a ranch some miles from town, and kept a double-barreled shotgun handy for any young man who dared to try to call on them. But he was an enthusiastic lodge member and once a month he went to Sacramento to lodge meeting. Then a couple of the boys took a case of beer out to the Casey ranch, and they had quite a party. But as nearly as the story teller could remember, old man Casey wouldn't be due to go to Sacramento again for several days. Too bad.

The friendly Benician, eager to do the best he could for the sporty stranger, would ask everyone who dropped in to loaf in the hotel lobby if he could think of any excitement for a visitor, but none could for perhaps twenty minutes. Then an innocent-looking good actor would stroll in without seeing the stranger and his Benicia companion and ask the clerk:

"How'd it happen old man Casey went to Sac today? He ain't due to go there till next week, is he?"

"Dunno, egzackly," the clerk would reply in a stage whisper. "Sumpun special came up. But keep it dark. He don't want nobody to know he's gone."

Half an hour later, a livery rig containing the city slicker and the friendly Benician would drive up to a sequestered ranch house, unload a case of beer and other provisions, and tell the driver to return about midnight. But as the rig drove away a fierce giant armed with a double-barreled shotgun appeared, and the city slicker and the Benician fled in different directions. Shots rang out, the Benician screamed "I give up!" and the stranger moved on at record-breaking speed. Once he was out of sight, the confederates of the Benician came out of the brush to enjoy the refreshments for which the fleeing one had paid. The trick became known throughout the San Francisco Bay area as the Casey Run. The Casey girls were wholly imaginary.

In the Mojave and Colorado deserts, which really are one, the lone prospector with his laden mule or burro may still be seen, for the mule or burro can go many places even a jeep cannot. Every little desert town has its "desert rats," who seem to have no other occupation besides prospecting and who somehow make a living at it. Mostly they are rather secretive and rarely volunteer much information except when more or less influenced by bottled conviviality, but anyone who asks them supercilious questions is likely to hear some marvelous tales of latest developments at Daggett or Ryolite or Calico or some other place, which once was rich with gold but has been robbed of everything except traditions. Most of the stories are not inspired by malice but are offered as entertainment. But if some dude-ranch guest from far away swallows them hook, line, and sinker it is a tribute to the raconteur's art, and a thing his fellow desert rats chuckle over, so that the aura of local fame sheds its glory on him.

That is only fair, for many of the guests who flee Chicago, New York, and Boston to spend the winter at desert resorts look on all the desert rats and other quaint characters as among the things provided for their amusement—which, quite frequently, they are—and if the natives can have fun at the expense of the visitors, they are only returning the compliment.

What is more, they return it with interest, proving that city slickers are more gullible than country bumpkins ever were. This, for example, is reported as authentic: A big car full of visitors and driven by a smug Angeleno—than whom no one can be smugger—drew up at Indio for a glass of grapefruit juice. Seeing a bewhiskered, innocent-looking desert rat, the driver questioned him for the entertainment of his guests:

"Grandpa, you look like you know this country. What's going on around here?"

The two women and the other men in the car were leaning forward, smiling to one another at this quaint and curious creature they were studying. Quite evidently they were tourists from the Middle West. The desert rat looked them over so mildly as to put them wholly off guard before he drawled:

"Ain't nothin' goin' on today. You should 'a' been here yistiddy."

"What went on yesterday?"

"Auto races at Salton Sea. Some of the best auto racers from L.A."

"You don't say? Where could they find a place to race there?"

"Oh, they jist tore through cactus and greasewood when they had to. But mostly the sand was purty smooth."

"Who won?"

"That was the funny thing. Young feller from Mecca, in his old battered-up Ford, beat 'em all."

"You mean he beat the big professional racers from Los Angeles?" demanded the driver incredulously.

"Yep. He sure did."

"How did that happen?"

"He jist knowed the country better, I reckon."

"What happened?"

"It was so hot the light oil burnt right out of the bearin's of the city fellers' cars, but the Mecca boy got some of that dry ice they make over at Niland an' his car picked up jist like it would on a frosty mornin', once it got warmed up."

"You don't mean to tell me some of the country's greatest car racers didn't take everything into consideration?"

"Oh, they caught on pretty quick. But they never would 'a' got near the Mecca boy if it hadn't been for the cholla. He run over that cactus an' punctured all four tires."

"How could he win after that?"

"Well, he jist happened to see a nest o' rattlesnakes right ahead and he run smack into 'em. They bit all the tires an' they swelled up so fast you'd never of knowed anything had happened. So the Mecca boy won by a good ten feet."

The desert rat looked innocent and simple-minded. The two women and the other men murmured ejaculations but looked to the driver. He wasn't sure what to do and looked suspiciously at a package under the desert rat's right arm.

"What are you going to do with all that whisky, Grandpa?" he demanded.

"Do with it?" repeated the desert man mildly. "Why, what's one quart of whisky among one?"

Then one of the listening group near by snickered, and the interrogator drove on with his guests.

That kind of tall tale looks like the direct offspring of Dan De Quille's story of solar armor, a rubber suit equipped with a compressor and batteries, by means of which the wearer could make himself hot or cold by merely pressing a button. It was a wonderful invention but was lost to science because the brave inventor started across Death Valley to prove its efficacy. With the cold turned on he could laugh at a temperature of 140 degrees, but he was never again seen alive. When found he was frozen, with an icicle eighteen inches long hanging from his nose. Apparently he had been unable to turn off the cold and had given his life for science.

That impossible story caused chuckles throughout the mining camps in the sixties just as did the story of Darius Green and his flying machine whenever it was written. Now the flying machine is an essential of modern existence, and the late war brought electrically heated "armor" into actual use.

George McCarthy, owner of a guest ranch near Victorville, has entranced many visitors with his story of the canteen fish. One always has to drag the story out of George. I once tried to get him to tell it to Aldous Huxley, but he shook his head sadly and reproachfully.

"No," he said. "Some folks who don't know our valley think it's just a made-up story, and that sorter hurts my feelin's."

This is the story:

George and a partner had been prospecting in the desert till they were far from any road or any other human habitation—or any water. They had built a little shack and were working toward the mouth of a canyon opening out of the mountains, on the theory that the rains and snows of many generations had washed gold down from the mountains. They knew torrents had come out of that canyon mouth at some time, because there was a deep sink in the desert which undoubtedly had been cut by those streams of long ago. But the two prospectors were miles from the nearest water hole, and all the "liquid silver" they had was in a barrel. (In the desert, "liquid silver" means water.) That barrel was their most carefully guarded treasure, for the water hole from which they had brought the water was drying up.

They knew they should turn back, but they had found traces of gold and could not till they were down to their last two canteens of water. They were about to give up and return to their shack when they found a little nugget in some gravel. Then they became feverish with excitement. They went on and found some coarse gold in the sand, and then on and on, lured by small but shining pockets of promise.

They had used up all the water in their canteens, and the sun was sinking behind the encircling mountains, before they realized that they were far from their shack and very close to dangerous thirst, and that if darkness caught them they might get lost.

They built a marker of such stones, greasewood, and cactus as they could gather in a hurry and turned back. Then one of the sudden storms which occasionally burst in the mountains blotted out the canyon above them. Realizing that a cloudburst up there might mean a flood in the broad sink in which they had been panning, they hurried. But they were still in the middle of the sink when the flash flood was on them. A wall of water higher than their heads roared down on them and hurled them ahead of it, swimming for their lives. Their situation was desperate, but they were hardy men. Their effort was to keep afloat and let the flood carry them till its force diminished.

They were swimming so when George's outstretched hand closed on something slippery and wriggly. Fearing it might be a rattlesnake, he flung it from him so violently that it landed on the bank, which was dry, as all the rain had fallen in the mountains above them. But as he flung it he saw it was not a snake but a fish. Then both men found themselves in the midst of a veritable school of fish, which apparently were even more helpless in the flood than they were.

The fish swarmed about them, climbing on them. By that time the men had managed to drift toward the side of the sink on which they had made camp and found they were in shallower water. Though the flood was still rushing down the sink, they could touch bottom and could see the way to safety.

Still the fish eddied around them, as purposeful as swarming bees. Thinking a fine fish fry would be good for supper, they began grasping them with both hands and hurling them out on to the bank.

The situation had been so dramatic George hadn't stopped to wonder at the miracle of a school of fish in the desert, but at last, almost exhausted, he called:

"We got more'n we can eat in a week. Let's get

out. I've heard of it rainin' fish, but darned if this ain't the first time I ever believed it."

"These didn't come from the sky," said his partner. "These are canteen fish."

"What are canteen fish?"

"You don't find 'em anywhere except in the Mojave," said the other. "They live in the little water holes scattered through the desert, and they're sort of queer shaped. Each one has a hump on its back like a camel, which it can fill with water. That's its canteen, and they always carry a reserve supply. They have some strange way of knowin' when a water hole is goin' to dry up and before it does they all fill their canteens and start off across the desert to some bigger water hole. Guess they can smell water twenty miles away. They march in a regular column, flippin' along on their tails. These poor fish must 'a' been crossin' the sink when the flood hit 'em. They're not used to anything but shallow water, like you'd find around some desert spring, and if it hadn't been for us they'd have all been drowned."

So George and his partner, full of pity, kept on throwing the fish out onto the bank until they had tossed out hundreds. By that time George had noticed that each one did have a queer hump or tank on its back. The fish kept struggling toward the two men instead of striving to elude them, but many were swept away by the turgid waters, and George could not help feeling full of sympathy for them as he saw the despair in their eyes as they were carried out of reach.

When at last the two men climbed out of the sink their sympathy for the creatures whose lives they had saved made it impossible to kill and eat any of them. By that time the water was receding rapidly, and soon the desert, they knew, would swallow it up. So they ran to the sink, filled their canteens, and ran with them to their shack. They emptied them into the barrel and ran back for more water. If they could only get enough water in that barrel to wash out some of the gold, they believed their fortunes would be made. But by that time the water was being blotted up by the sand so rapidly that it was only a forlorn hope.

As they carried back their refilled canteens, and a bucket they had had in the shack, with another load of water, they realized they were leading a procession. All the canteen fish, flipping along on their tails, were following them. The men exchanged ejaculations of surprise but hurried on, having no time to do more than vaguely wonder. But as they emptied their canteens into the barrel the riddle solved itself. The leaders of the fish parade flipped up on top of things piled beside the shack till they reached the level of the barrel-top and emptied their canteens into it. All the other fish followed suit, after which they happily flipped away to the vanishing stream to refill their canteens and bring back more.

"They'd caught on to the fact that we wanted that water mighty bad," George says, "and were so darned grateful to us for savin' their lives they wanted to show their appreciation."

One evening George told that story to a room full of guests from the Middle West, maintaining such an air of grave and simple honesty no one knew whether to laugh or not. They looked to those who were California-wise for guidance, but they gave no sign. After a long pause a woman from Chicago asked:

"But, Mr. McCarthy, did you get the gold?"

"Yes, ma'am," averred George solemnly. "That's how I bought this ranch."

Maybe it was stories like that which made Henry Watterson say: "In California every man is a damned liar." And maybe those who knew that the strangers had found the desert such an unearthly place they could believe almost anything about it, should not have abetted George in such barefaced deception. But tall tales are an old California custom. And no doubt before their stay was out those same guests were urging George to hoax other newcomers with that same story.

IT IS doubtful if any other section of the world of comparable area has been harried by real-estate speculation to the extent that California has. The Spanish settlers didn't have to worry about land. There was plenty, and whether or not one had a land grant no one was going to object to one's living on some of it. That was a great help to many of the first settlers from the United States, for they squatted on the Spaniards' lands and never gave them up. But even then there was plenty of land that no one claimed, and there still is.

The Spaniards subdivided only for their families or their friends. John Bidwell is authority for the statement that owners of great ranches often gave fifty or one hundred acres to some friend who had done them a service. As far as records go, Villa de Branciforte was the only "model town" the Spaniards planned, and there the land was allotted and given, since the settlers were too poor to buy any. It faded from the map in a short while, though much of it is in the present site of Santa Cruz. All the other Spanish towns just grew. People built their houses wherever they chose without any idea of a townsite plat. When streets or trails among them became necessary, they simply followed the paths pedestrians and horsemen—mainly horsemen —had made.

But the Yanks were subdividers from the word go. We have already seen how, after the gold strike at Weaverville, the land anyone could have had for the taking before was cut up into lots which sold at $800 apiece, and they weren't very big lots. The squatters who virtually stole land from the great Peralta rancho also cut it up into townsites and sold lots in what now are the cities of Oakland, Berkeley, and Alameda. But the first subdivider in California—the first who platted a townsite and filed maps of it and advertised it as a community for homeseekers—was one Henry Meiggs, who platted an addition to San Francisco which he called North Beach. Yerba Buena had been created in 1839 by order of Governor Alvarado and in 1844 had only twelve houses and fifty inhabitants. In 1847, its name was changed to San Francisco by order of its alcalde, to the great annoyance of the neighboring community of Francisca, which was just starting and had been named in honor of Doña Francisca Benicia Carrillo Vallejo, wife of General Mariano Vallejo.

There was bitter rivalry between the communities then, for Robert Semple had declared that Yerba Buena was no place for a settlement and that Francisca was going to be the really important city. He was so outraged by Yerba Buena's appropriation of a name almost duplicating that of Francisca that he forthwith changed the name of his town to Benicia, which was Señora Vallejo's middle name. But San Francisco began to grow, and no doubt Meiggs appealed to all its patriotic pride with his promises for a subdivision which would surpass any other residence area on the Pacific.

Like many a subdivider who came after him, Meiggs was eloquent with alluring promises of what he was going to do and gathered in quite a few down payments. He promised so much more than he could make good that, the early American settlers of San Francisco being what they were, he decided it would be much healthier for him in the South Seas than within bullet range of any of those who had put out money for lots in North Beach, and unobtrusively left on an outward-bound ship.

It was well for him—and, as it turned out, for others—that he did so, for warrants for his arrest had been issued. Yet he has gone into history as exceptional among the tricky subdividers of California, for after the South Seas he went to South America, made a fortune in Peru and Chile as a railroad builder, and made such a sincere effort to make restitution to those who had lost money on his venture that the legislature of 1873-74 passed a measure granting him amnesty. But that measure was passed over the veto of Governor Newton Booth, and Meiggs was so afraid Governor Booth and other irreconcilables would find some way to punish him that he never came back. He died in Lima.

Benicia was still in there pitching. In 1848, Semple and others assured the world it was to be the capital of the West, and two hundred lots were sold at an average price of eighteen dollars a lot. When California was admitted as a state in 1850, Benicia set out to become the capital. Monterey had been the Spanish and Mexican capital most of the time and was the first American seat of government. But Benicia shouted its claims so loudly that in May, 1853, the legislature made it the capital, and it triumphantly raised money to build a capitol. That solid little building, as we have seen, is still in use. It is about big enough for a city hall in a town of five thousand, but it was big enough for California then. At that time, however, Placerville, which had been named Hangtown before, was a city of forty thousand, and many other Mother Lode towns which now are only villages were bustling communities, much larger than Benicia, and the next February the legislature reversed itself and made Sacramento the capital, leaving Benicia's biggest building vacant, the empty shell of its dreams.

At that time southern California was cut off from northern California by mountains through which there were no roads, for the Camino Real connecting the missions was only a horse trail. By counting in all the outlying ranchers, Los Angeles could claim a population of two thousand, mostly Mexicans. But after 1860 Los Angeles began to grow as if it lived entirely on hormones and vitamins. In the eighties, when the Santa Fe built into Los Angeles, came the railroad war which probably wasn't a war at all. The Santa Fe and the Southern Pacific kept cutting rates till one could travel from the

Missouri River to California for one dollar—but couldn't get a return ticket for any such price. The railroads realized they had to have population in the West to make their business profitable. When people settled on the millions of acres the rail companies had been given by the federal government and the states as bonuses for building the roads, they would have both passengers and freight to carry. The public swallowed the bait so greedily that hundreds of thousands of people poured into California, and the lure of palms and roses took most of them to southern California.

Then Los Angeles became the center of such real-estate trading as had probably never been seen elsewhere. Land acquired for as little as fifteen cents an acre was subdivided and sold for fifty dollars a lot, then for a hundred, then for two hundred, five hundred, a thousand. The mere fact that it was worth only pennies yesterday made the gamblers sure it would be worth bags of gold tomorrow. The railroads joined in by sponsoring ornate hotels in areas in which there hadn't even been villages before, believing that the hotels would be the nuclei of thriving towns—and in many cases they were, for a while, at least.

Wherever one of those projects started, the subdividers went and let their visions run riot. Special trains were run to them. Tallyhos and carriage trains conveyed the newcomers to the nearer ones. The homeseekers were met with bands, were feasted, were entertained by music and Spanish dancers, and then the ablest orators purchasable pleaded with them to make their own and their descendants' future secure by investing in those lands, which undoubtedly would be selling for three times as much next week. The orators wore silk hats and long coats morning, noon, and night. They could point at numerous outstanding community leaders who had come to southern California with little or nothing and had become rich men by investing a few hundred dollars in real estate. And anyone could do it, for all you had to pay was a little down and a little every month.

"We hired the most imaginative liars we could find," one man who came in the eighties said, "but had to fire some of them because they couldn't come up to the truth. With the population doubling or trebling every decade, things happened which made their wildest visions fall short of the mark. Where I came from you couldn't sell property for residences unless it lay flat or was at least in a semi-reclining position, but here you could sell them lots that stood on end. And blessed if they didn't find ways of building houses on two or three levels which became a sort of fad. Today in some of our most exclusive residence districts you can drive into a garage on the street level, and then take an elevator straight down two or three floors to the living room or dining room, and then walk out on a terraced garden continuing to the bottom of a canyon."

That may take the breath away from the average resident of the plains states, but many of those canyon-side homes are charming to the eyes, whether or not they are friendly to the legs. In a thirty-room house with adequate elevator service it might be fine, but a six-room or eight-room house four stories tall must present some housekeeping difficulties. Carrie Jacobs Bond lived in a small house which was on three levels, and you had to go upstairs one flight from the front door. For the convenience of those who did not like to climb stairs, and her own convenience in her later years, Mrs. Bond had an elevator chair, which she could send down to the front door by pressing a button and bring up by pressing another. It ran along beside the stairs, and one felt almost as if one were sliding down the banister in a chair. And one touch of clever novelty makes the whole world kin. Once a small group there included Dr. Robert A. Millikan and Walt Disney, and both the great scientist and the famous maker of cartoons inspected the chair-elevator with bright-eyed interest.

The southern California boom burst in 1887.

Thousands of persons went back to their home states, selling out for nothing. People who had stood in line all night to be among the first to buy lots in new subdivisions and new towns, which existed only on paper, cursed California and let their property go for taxes. Just as northern California miners had rushed to every place at which a new gold strike was reported, southern California real-estate speculators had rushed to every new community that was announced with glittering promises and seemed to have some big interest back of it. They had been ready to believe that paradise plus riches was just around the corner, but as soon as the boom burst they were equally convinced that all that was in store for Los Angeles was hell plus poverty. There are still plenty of old-timers in Los Angeles who can tell you how they were offered the land on which the City Hall now stands for $250, or other properties now worth millions for comparable sums.

But the tide had started pouring in, and nothing could stop it. Despite the thousands who gave up in despair and went away saying Los Angeles and southern California were finished, in 1890 the population was twice what it had been in 1885, in 1900 it had doubled again. by 1910 it had trebled since 1900, and today its city planners confidently assure you it will be a city of six million in another

quarter century—and its realtors are just as eloquent in assuring you that properties bought now
will guarantee your future as their predecessors
were fifty years ago. And they are all so generous
they want you to get rich instead of holding the
land and getting rich themselves.

Up to the time of tire and gas rationing, the free
sightseeing bus, which took you out to see the
homes of the movie stars, was a familiar sight. It
did take you past the homes of movie stars, or homes
which looked as if they might be the homes of
movie stars, and frequently some man or woman
too far away to be recognized was pointed out to the
gapers as some world-famous person. And as you
rode along, the guide, a benevolent-looking gentleman with graying hair, told you how, when he was
a young man, he used to hunt rabbits on Wilshire
Boulevard and there was nothing but a field of wild
oats at Hollywood and Vine, humorously adding
that a good many wild oats of a different kind had
been sown there since. "I had the chance," he
would say sadly, "to buy that piece of property
right there for $1,600, but I was just a smart aleck
then and turned it down. Last week it sold for
$1,200,000 " And then at last you came to the ad-
dition which was sure to outshine all the rest, and
your guide got really eloquent. With tears in his
eyes he pictured the sorrows that came to those

who did not prepare for their future, the sudden illness that left the widow and the darling little baby penniless, forgetting to say that at such times those who couldn't meet their time payments were likely to find the mortgage foreclosed. He painted such pictures of the happiness, the health, the joy, and the nine-hundred-per-cent profit anyone who bought in that subdivision was sure to reap that honeymooning brides began whispering to their young husbands. In such states as Kentucky, where every man is an orator by instinct, they love to lay it on thick at funerals, for instance, but nowhere else has the tremolo been used as effectively as by the orators employed to lecture to crowds taken to Los Angeles subdivisions.

Once a young fellow out of a job begged five of us to take the trip because he got fifty cents a head for the adults he could get to take it. We were given a truly delightful drive and much information which was interesting if not always true. Even so it compared very well with what one learns on the average sight-seeing bus. Then we were given an excellent luncheon, with entertainment while we ate. And then the orator of the day took the platform, and the waters came down at Lodore. We sat there awed, convinced that in Mississippi or South Carolina that man could have been elected a United States Senator without even trying, yet when he gestured dramatically we could see that his cuffs were frayed. His logic seemed faultless, his evidence compelling, his benevolence beyond all question. He was only seeking our good, not anything for himself. And we felt ashamed, for all of us had just come along for the ride.

We had come in busses, though, and couldn't get away till the busses left. After the oration we were sought out, in a most complimentary way, and asked if we wouldn't be introduced to Mr. Skite. After all, it was the least we could do. We had no idea who Mr. Skite was, but apparently we were indebted to him for some hours of entertainment and we would be glad to thank him.

Mr. Skite was what they called the closer. He must have studied hypnotism, for he made us feel that it was our solemn duty to our families, our country, and to him to pay forty-five hundred dollars each for lots which slanted like the roof of the house of seven gables, and the only thing that saved most of us from making fools of ourselves was that we didn't have any money. One member of the party was so unfortunate as to be able to write his check for five hundred dollars, and when he got out of the closer's office he had parted with it. He felt very sheepish, once he had recovered from the hypnotic spell the closer exerted, for he had no money to build on the lot he had bargained for.

But three years later he sold it for more than twice what it had cost him.

The realtors of southern California are so alert they turn everything to their advantage, even the Easter sunrise service. The first Easter sunrise service was held on Mount Roubidoux, near Riverside. Jacob Riis, Henry Van Dyke, and John Hendrick Bangs were guests at the Mission Inn in Riverside. Their host was Frank Miller, owner of the inn and devotee of literary and artistic achievement. Mr. Miller continually invited writers and artists to the inn as his guests. It was after seeing a sunset from Mount Roubidoux that Carrie Jacobs Bond wrote "The End of a Perfect Day." Joseph C. Lincoln wrote a book there. John Steven McGroarty's *Mission Play* was written while the author was a guest there, and many noted authors and artists have spent weeks or months there as Mr. Miller's guests. Unfortunately for authors and artists, Mr. Miller has passed on.

It was the night before Easter when Riis, Van Dyke, and Bangs were there, and one of them said they should remember the day in some way. Miller suggested that the best way would be to go to the top of Mount Roubidoux and have Van Dyke read his poem, "God of the Out of Doors," and the four decided to do that. A few other guests went along, and the simplicity and beauty of that celebration made a pretty story for the newspapers. Marcella Kraft, who had sung in grand opera, lived in Riverside, and the next year the sunrise service was more elaborate. All through Easter Eve the lights of approaching motor cars could be seen winding up to Mount Roubidoux, like an endless chain of fireflies. When the service began the whole mountainside was covered with spectators—it isn't a very big mountain—and when it ended many who never had seen the world from an eminence at daybreak took time to look out on it and be stirred by its clean freshness and beautiful serenity.

This was not overlooked by the subdividers. Every one who had what was classed as "view property" wondered if he couldn't attract a throng to admire its beauty by holding a sunrise service there. Near San Diego a mountain estates subdivision was platted, and Madam Schumann-Heink was the first person offered strong inducements to locate there. The first thing laid out there was the place for the sunrise service, commanding stirring views in all directions. It was all done with reverence and solemnity, but it was hoped many of those attracted by the service would be impressed both by the beauty of their surroundings and the quality of those who had built or intended to build in that subdivision. At the first service one cynic summed it up thus: "This is the first time I ever saw a subdivision opened with prayer."

There is one very bad result of the addiction of southern Californians to gambling in real estate. They are among the most restless people on earth, often deceived by their own deception. As one disgusted Angeleno put it, "The trouble with this town is that everybody's got one foot in the stirrup." Hundreds of thousands of persons are less interested in creating homes to live in than homes to sell. If you visit a charming place, in which you would expect the owners to wish to spend the rest of their lives, you dare not get enthusiastic about it lest they try to sell it to you. Literally thousands of persons have made either a vocation or an avocation of buying places, improving them artistically, and selling at a profit of a few thousand dollars. Such persons always go to the new subdivisions, the ones most virulently advertised, abandoning good neighbors and old friends to live among people of whom they know nothing, but who have all the appearance of being swank. An oak has to grow a long time in one place to become a great oak. The persons who never take root can never draw much sustenance from the soil they own, no matter where it is. They are sustained by atmosphere alone, which cannot give enduring strength to either individuals or communities.

A noted motion-picture writer lived in a beautiful neighborhood in Beverly Hills. Next door lived a charming family, as neighborly as if they lived in a country town. The adults and their children found pleasure in their daily contacts. But the family next door was offered such a profit on their home they felt they could not refuse it—though they did not need the money—and moved away. The people who moved into the house had two beautiful cars and beautiful furniture. The people next door went to the hedge dividing the properties with an offer of the use of their telephone or anything like that which might be required and were thanked courteously. Shortly afterward they were called on.

"There's one thing you can do for us, if you will," said the man. "Come over and help us have a sort of housewarming. We've got some cocktails all ready."

That was rather hurrying things. But the "old residents" never had been bitten by a cocktail and, as they were sitting in a lawn swing, could not plead other engagements. They accepted the invitation and, of course, had to reciprocate by inviting the new neighbors to their own house, where they introduced them to a number of friends.

A week or so later they were startled by gunfire. The pleasant new neighbor next door was a na-

tionally known gangster, wearing an alias, and the
F.B.I. had tracked him down.

That was in one of the most "exclusive" neigh-
borhoods in California, where the prices of property
excluded most persons, and it was due to the fact
that nearly everyone in southern California is more
or less in the real-estate business. That is, nearly
everyone figures on what profit he could sell out for
and what he could do with the money in some
other neighborhood. The homestead handed down
from generation to generation is almost unknown.
If the second generation doesn't feel it imperative
to sell at some peak and move to the new neighborhood that is the fad of the moment, the third generation is sure to want to tear down the old place
and build a new, modernistic bandbox, with a rum-
pus room and bar, which might appropriately be
named Pushbutton Manor.

And it isn't all the fault of the rising generations.
Since infancy they have heard tall tales of how
much Mr. Blank or Mrs. Null has cleaned up by
selling and moving, until the idea that home is just
a piece of merchandise has taken hold of their
minds. The habit of gauging all real property by
its money value rather than by its sentimental or
spiritual value is an old California custom which is
bad for the soul and weakening to the character.

The astonishing thing is that Californians can

more easily convince themselves than they can convince newcomers from other states that new subdivisions and new towns are going to be all that the sellers promise. They can believe in miracles because they have seen so many. Perhaps forty years ago, a St. Louis doctor thought of establishing a sort of health resort in the Colorado Desert and was offered everything in and around one place he visited for ten thousand dollars. They couldn't fool a man from Missouri. He would have none of it. In the late thirties he visited that place again and rubbed his eyes. It was Palm Springs, which probably couldn't be bought today for a hundred million.

As Will Rogers put it, wayfarers across the desert still have to beware of the Escrow Indians. Immediately following World War II, subdividers broke out on the desert again. They acquired government land and bought up railroad lands—some of the alternate sections given the railroads as bonuses for building. Much of the land cost them less than three dollars an acre. They platted it, developed some water, laid out streets, townsites, magnificent hotels, and clubhouses—all on paper—and soon were selling the land at fifteen dollars an acre, then at fifty, then at a hundred, then for five hundred and a thousand in some cases. Yet within a mile of some of that land one could still homestead government land just as good except for the improvements.

But all the buyers are figuring that each new desert area in which they are buying is destined to be another Palm Springs, though each is only one of several such places in the Colorado and Mojave Deserts.

And the buyers are not mainly persons from other states whose health compels them to live in an arid climate. They are people from Santa Monica, Long Beach, San Diego, and other seacoast towns, for whom an area with an average annual rainfall of only half an inch is a complete change. Those who can afford it buy acres or lots and put up week-end cottages, to which they can get away in winter and be reasonably sure of warmth and sunshine. Others just hang on to their lots, waiting for the dawn of the era of high prices. But practically all of them buy with the idea that they can enjoy the place a few years and then sell out at a profit. That is what Californians have been doing for more than a hundred years, and they have got so into the habit of it that each new generation regards it as a birthright.

F ROM earliest times, Californians have cherished fairy tales and handed them down to succeeding generations which accepted them as gospel and grew belligerent in their defense. The first explorers were lured by the legend that California was an island of amazons and jewels. Coronado's search for the Seven Cities of Cibola was inspired by a Spanish legend which had nothing to do with America, yet it brought ecstatic visions to the viceroy as well as to the common soldier. And from those days to the present there never has been a time when many Californians were not wagering all they possessed on the truth of fantastic promises of riches, health, or heaven held out to them by crackpots or charlatans.

There's hardly a stenographer or ribbon clerk in California who hasn't bought a share or two of stock in gold mines or oil wells which never got past the promotion stage, or hasn't made a payment or two on desert or mountain land so inaccessible most of them never expect to see it, or hasn't "given" liberally to some cultist whose theories and methods seem utterly ridiculous or fraudulent to most persons, yet who is living in affluence because of the credulity of a host of followers.

The very name of California is one of the things about which innumerable Californians believe what isn't true. Hanna's *Dictionary of California Land Names* says the name had been a topic of speculation ever since the discovery of what now is Lower California in 1533. Captain Frederick William Beachey, English explorer, seems to have been the first to advance the theory, in 1826, that the name came from the Latin words *calida* and *fornax* "signifying heat and furnace." That became a popular opinion with students. The friars spoke Latin, and many had come to California by way of deserts in which they endured terrific heat. The students of 120 years ago who accepted that belief handed it down, and in California anything which comes from an ancestor that far back is accepted as having come straight from the horse's mouth.

But Mariano Vallejo and Juan B. Alvarado asserted that the name came from the Lower California Indian word *Kali-forno*, meaning high hill or native land, though it is pretty hard to prove there ever was such an Indian word. When Coronado asked Indians if the Seven Cities lay just beyond, the Indians said they did because they thought that was the answer he wanted, and if later Indians were asked if they had ever used such a word as *Kali-forno* they probably cheerfully agreed to that, too.

The debate seems to have gone on intermittently from 1533 to 1862. The Jesuit historian Miguel Venegas discussed it in 1757, as did Francisco Clavijero in 1789. Greek and Latin scholars put in their theories, the Latins arguing for *Calidas Fornus*, *Calienta Fornalia*, and such, and the Greeks for *Kala Phor Nea* and *Kala Chorn Nea*. But in 1862, asserts Mr. Hanna, the distinguished antiquarian Edward Everett Hale "solved the origin of the name to the satisfaction of all." The romantic novel *Las Sergas de Esplandian* had told of a mythical island named "California," inhabited by amorous ama-

zons and fairly bubbly with pearls, and the chances
are that Cortez and many of his officers had heard
of that alluring island. It may have been compar-
atively as well known among those explorers
as Shangri-la became to American expeditionary
forces in the Orient during World War II.

Yet Mr. Hanna was overoptimistic in concluding
that the Hale discovery had settled the argument to
the satisfaction of all. One could hardly expect a
descendant of Mariano Vallejo or Juan Alvarado to
believe that any Yankee could know more about
the origin of the name of California than did the
Spaniards who settled and developed it, so there
you are.

The *Calida Fornax* legend seems logical enough
in desert areas and is told authoritatively to tourists
who gulp it down without a blink. Mr. Hanna has
received hot letters asserting that great-grandpapa
should know for he was there, and he said *Kali-
forno* was an Indian word. Thus, thousands of Californians hold fast to their ancient privilege of
believing what isn't true.

One of the favorite customs of Spanish California
was to attribute almost miraculous powers to the
waters of certain springs. As every early settler was
eager for offspring, the waters of several were
asserted to be conducive to reproductiveness. The
most famous of those springs was El Polin, on the

lands of the Miramontes family, not far from what
was then the little presidio to protect Yerba Buena.
"Polin" was said to be an Indian name, and the
legend is supposed to have come from the Indians,
who may have heard that some of the Spaniards
were seeking a Fountain of Youth. "The spring,"
says Davis' *Sixty Years in California,* "was celebrated from a very remote period for its virtues,
which were handed down from the Indians for
generations. It was claimed that it possessed the remarkable power of producing fecundity in women
who were childless. Many authentic instances could
be quoted in support of this assertion. The Miramontes family had twenty children and other
families living in the neighborhood were blessed
with a large progeny. Many who came to the place
from a distance, by the advice of friends, to test the
wonderful qualities of the water were later rewarded for their faith by a happy increase in their
families. The first wife of Willam D. M. Howard,
a well known early San Franciscan, for several
years without children, went thither by the advice
of Mrs. Miramontes, and at the proper time was
blessed with a daughter."

That was only one of many cases, the more notable of which were those of couples who were parents to from twenty to thirty-six children. The
waters were supposed to be as beneficial to men

as to women. If we remember that Yerba Buena and the first presidio were established to hold the land by right of possession against possible Russian encroachment, some will conclude the whole legend may have been concocted to inspire settlers to move there, and men to seek service in the adjacent military post. Similarly, when Sonoma had been created to hold the land "against Russians and other foreigners," but could muster only forty families for that patriotic purpose, the story went out that three pairs of twins and one set of triplets had been born there, all because of the climate and the water.

Such stories are reported in California's most authentic histories, and though everyone smiles at them it is an interesting fact that, when a statewide gathering of members of E. Clampus Vitus met in San Francisco in 1947, several thousand small bottles of ordinary city water were sold at fifty cents each, all because the label on them asserted they were filled with water from El Polin.

Stories of extreme longevity are among other things Californians have always been glad to repeat, even when they didn't believe them, invariably inspiring friends and relatives to broadcast the stories dogmatically because of such firsthand information. Eulalia Perez, who died in 1877 while dictating her recollections, assured her friends she was 139 years old, though when it was polite to do so doubting Thomases whispered that she was only 118.

One of California's most cherished falsehoods asserts that the reason the tiles on the old missions were smaller at one end than at the other was that when the padres had the Indians make the tiles they were molded over the Indians' thighs. Recently an elderly native son, whose father was a pioneer of Los Angeles, made that statement before a meeting of the Westerners, an organization of lovers of Western history, and most of those present nodded their heads. They had all heard that story from their forbears. A company which does a national business in building tiles employed researchers to write a booklet about tiles, and the researchers accepted that statement unthinkingly. If one stops to think, the story is ridiculous. The tiles on the old missions ranged from eighteen to twenty-two inches in length, and no known human thigh was ever that long. The tiles on a roof could not have fitted together so as to keep out rain had they been molded on the thighs of many different Indians, even if giants could have been found with thighs long enough to mold an eighteen-inch tile between the knee and the crotch.

The fact is that the first missions built in California had thatched roofs. Many of the Indians rebelled against the benevolent assimilation of the missions and went on the warpath. San Luis Obispo Mission was burned out three times, for the Indians soon learned what flaming arrows could do to a thatched roof. That was the necessity which mothered the invention of the mission tile. The padres realized they must have roofs which could not be set afire. The tiles were made smaller at one end than at the other for the same reason that shingles are thinner on one end than on the other, so that each lower row will fit snugly under the row above it. All the other missions adopted the San Luis Obispo invention, and the wooden molds on which the tiles were made are preserved at several of them.

Another story which will not down is about the name of Azusa. A famous syndicated columnist, traveling through California, once wrote that the name signified "from A to Z, the best in U.S.A." That is one of the things that make one wonder how many other incorrect statements made by famous columnists are treasured as truth in the minds of many persons. The fact is that the name is of Indian origin, long antedating the time when California was part of the United States. Roger Dalton, whose English grandfather became Don Enrique Dalton and the owner of Rancho Azusa Dalton, on a small part of which the present city of Azusa stands, testifies that the Mexican land grants issued

after the secularization of the mission lands desig-
nated the region by the Indian name, and it is so
recorded in the record books of the 1830's. Probably
it was the poetic touch of a chamber-of-commerce
booster that resulted in the "A to Z in U.S.A." legend, for the real meaning of that pretty name is
not quite so alluring. The real meaning is "skunk
hill."

La Jolla, lovely suburb of San Diego, is another
community that clings belligerently to a legend for
which there is no discoverable foundation. In Spanish, "j" is pronounced "h" and "ll" is pronounced
"y". Thus La Jolla is called La Hoya. There is also
the Spanish word *joya*, meaning jewel, which is
pronounced "hoya." The chances are that when the
community was named someone who knew how
"j" and "ll" are pronounced in Spanish named it
La Jolla, thinking he was calling it "the jewel,"
though the correct spelling would have been La
Joya. However, it's an old American custom not to
admit a mistake if one can get out of it, and some
La Jollans stoutly aver the name is old Spanish,
while others as vigorously assert the name is
Indian, meaning "the caves."

In San Diego, thousands of Californians, among
others, annually pay to visit "Ramona's Marriage
Place," and up to a few years ago California newspapers frequently published pictures of an aging

Indian woman living on a reservation near San Jacinto who was said to have been the original Ramona. In Monterey they tell you of the rose-tree trysting place of the lovely girl named Nachita and young Lieutenant William Tecumseh Sherman. When things get dull in Sacramento printshops, one of them is likely to bring out a pamphlet of ribald verses credited to Black Bart, which numerous collectors of California buy and treasure. But all the evidence indicates Ramona was a fictitious or composite character; the aged woman who was Nachita assured Mrs. Sanchez that she never had met Lieutenant Sherman and that the whole legend of her romance was a myth; and, after the most thorough study of Black Bart's career anyone has made, Joseph Henry Jackson says the only poetic effort which can be charged to Black Bart is the quatrain quoted in our chapter about bandits. It's just an old California custom to create romantic legends and believe them after they have become popular.

Yet one of them, the story of an Indian curse, affected so many superstitious persons that action had to be taken. When a Mexican grant was made to a great estate in San Diego County, it was provided that the Indians, who for generations had buried their dead near the hot springs there and bathed in the healing waters, should have that part of the ranch "perpetually." When the ranch came into American hands, the Indians were ordered off, and a company of soldiers was sent to move them. The Indians agreed to leave next morning and spent the whole night in a ceremony in which they invoked retribution on the white owners of the land. The first American manager of the ranch was riding over it when his horse stumbled in a gopher hole and he was killed. His successor also met accidental death, as did the third man to take charge of it. That caused so many persons to repeat the story of the Indian curse that few wanted any part of that ranch, and many were in such constant fear of chuck holes, rattlesnakes, falling trees, and other natural booby traps that they avoided the property as much as possible. That went on for decades, till Colonel Ed Fletcher, who had inspired many great real-estate developments in San Diego County, and who had won the friendship of the Indians, brought about a compromise. The owners of the ranch agreed to give the Indians their burying ground and let them hold their annual encampments around the hot springs, and in return the Indians held another solemn conclave—and revoked the curse!

Another favorite self-deception of Californians is that land they own or their ancestors owned was a grant "direct from the King of Spain." A realtor wishing to sell land to a movie star who has acquired the wish to become one of the landed gentry likes to say impressively: "There will have been only three changes of ownership between you and the King of Spain. The King granted this land to Don Luis Soandso in recognition of distinguished services and did it in a royal manner, picking out one of the most beautiful spots in California for his favorite." The fact is that all the land grants were made by governors of California, and the King of Spain never knew anything about them. But they were all made in the name of the King, for it was customary for the governors to do practically everything in the name of their King. W. W. Robinson's *Ranchos Become Cities* says that search of the records fails to show any grants direct from the King, and cites this verbatim evidence of the way grants of all kinds were made: In 1788 Governor Fages signed an official document which read: "In the royal name of His Majesty, I grant to the petitioner the use in right of ownership of the brand which he exhibits in order to mark his cattle." No one claims his cattle brand came direct from the King of Spain, though many were granted just like that. It was that same Governor Fages who made the first land grants in California, "in the royal name of His Majesty."

The readiness of Californians—and many other folk—to believe what isn't true brings us back to

the most fantastic story of the Magnificent Ralston.
When Ralston was looked on as the great financial
genius of the West, two simple miners entered the
Bank of California and asked if they could leave a
leather bag of stones in the vault for a day or two.
It was not unusual for miners to check bags of gold
dust in that way, but the bank teller thought a bag
of stones was different and asked what they were.
The miners didn't know for sure but thought maybe
they had something valuable. The teller looked and
found the bag full of uncut diamonds plus some
rubies and sapphires. He asked where the miners
had got them, and they said that was their business
but they had a forty-acre claim full of such stuff.
When they came back for their stones later they
were told Mr. Ralston would like to see them. They
were hesitant, but the teller had signaled Ralston,
and that affable gentleman took them into his private office. After worming their secret out of them,
Ralston told them that if their discovery was as stu-
pendous as it appeared it would take a $10,000,000
company properly to develop their claim. The miners didn't know anything about such big money,
but told Ralston that if he wanted they would sell
out for $660,000.

Ralston called in a few associates and some lapidaries. The latter agreed the stones were genuine
and estimated there were about fifty thousand dol-

lars' worth in the bag. Ralston agreed that, if As-
bury Harpending, mining engineer, inspected their
claim and found it all they said it was, he and his
associates would buy it. But in the meantime all
were pledged to secrecy.

Nothing so tremendous could be kept secret. With
the Mother Lode the greatest gold field ever found
up to that time, and the Comstock Lode the greatest
silver deposit, people were ready to believe anything of the West. Harpending was in London and
had to be sent for. A San Francisco newspaper in-
dignantly declared: "Ralston, Lent and Roberts
have hold of a remarkable source of wealth and refuse to let their fellow citizens share in it." Chicago
and New York financiers tried to get in on the
ground floor. As Harpending was about to sail from
England, Baron Rothschild called on him to see if
he couldn't acquire a financial interest in the
venture.

In the meantime, the two simple miners had
gone back to their claim to bring out more evidence
of what they had found. They returned just about
the time Harpending arrived. On the way out of
the mountains, they said, they had been caught in
a flash flood and had lost one bag of stones, but the
one they had saved made the eyes of two lapidaries
Ralston had employed bulge.

Besides Harpending, Ralston had summoned a

mining engineer named Jamin from New York.
The miners agreed to lead Harpending, Jamin, and
General George S. Dodge, a friend of Ralston, back
to their diggings.

They escorted them by train to Rawlins, Wyoming, and then took them on horseback for four
days. When they reached their forty acres they
said they were more than a hundred miles from
any railroad or sizable settlement. They let the in-
vestigators do their own investigating, and soon
Harpending found a diamond in an ant hill. Others
also found the stones. They returned to San Francisco and the lapidaries, and the reports bore out
the claims of the miners.

By that time the bitterness of the outsiders was
so great that Ralston agreed to let twenty-five leading citizens come into a stock company, each buying eighty thousand dollars' worth of stock. One of
the twenty-five was the representative of the Roth-
schilds.

One thing worried Harpending. While they were
inspecting the diamond field he thought he heard
the faint and far-off whistle of a train, and he
doubted if one could hear such a sound from a distance of more than twenty miles. He suspected the
miners of having led the party by a roundabout
route which had never taken them very far from

Rawlins. Such deception might be excusable under the circumstances, and it was hard to assume that two simple miners could have got hold of uncut diamonds the lapidaries thought would be worth more than one hundred thousand dollars when cut, but that train whistle worried him, though he had only half-heard it. He pursued the clue and found that the field really was only about twenty miles from Rawlins. Then he sent a geologist named King and an assistant named Berry to the diggings. They continued to find precious stones, but Berry found one which had been partly cut. A field which not only produced diamonds but cut them was too good for even Californians to believe in.

By that time all San Francisco was excited about diamonds. Several companies had been formed and were buying up leases on "diamond lands" in Wyoming. But when Ralston received a telegram from King, the incident known as "the great diamond hoax" ended.

Ralston made good the losses of many who had been caught by the swindle. *Ralston's Ring* credits him with the highest motives throughout. He had seen a chance to make San Francisco the diamond capital of the world and, as always, was ready to risk his wealth to do anything he dreamed was feasible for his beloved city. But probably that hoax was one of the things that shook national and international faith in Ralston's judgment and helped bring on his final tragedy.

At that time, however, Harpending seems to have been more bitter than Ralston. His professional reputation had been tarnished. He embarked on a search for the two miners. He found a London gem dealer who, two years before, had sold undergrade South African diamonds and a few rubies and sapphires to an American for $17,000. Eventually he traced one of the miners, a man named Arnold, to his home in Kentucky, and Arnold gave up $150,000. The other man, named Slack, never was located.

One Californian who did rather well by believing what wasn't true was "Emperor" Joshua Norton. Norton was a Forty-niner who amassed $250,000, it was said, but lost both his money and his reason when a bank failed in 1855. In his own eyes, though, he rose to dignity and pomp, and such was the generous sympathy of San Francisco that no one disillusioned him. He proclaimed himself Emperor of the United States and Defender of Mexico. He could go into stores and tailor shops and order things, and people would bow before him and say "Yes, Your Majesty." He wore a dazzling uniform of blue, with great gold epaulettes, and carried a shining sword. San Franciscans paid homage to him which was not mockery. Ralston even gave orders that his checks should be cashed. It is not on record that he was ever gibed or humiliated in public. If he walked into a theater, he was escorted to a box. If he called on Ralston or others of the great figures of San Francisco, he was courteously shown into private offices and treated with deference. There must be something in the soul of San Francisco that makes the average citizen more prone than most of us to say of the unfortunate: "There, but for the grace of God, go I."

The most grandiose monument to the readiness of Californians—and others—to believe what isn't true is Scotty's Castle in Death Valley, annually visited by thousands of tourists who go away convinced that it cost millions, and that Walter Scott must have found one of those fabulous lost mines for which so many have searched. Carl B. Glasscock carefully analyzed all the evidence in his book *Here's Death Valley*, and he also was very close to Albert M. Johnson, who really was "Scotty's" gold mine.

Even the birth dates Scott's closest relatives gave disagree with one another and with the date Scott himself has given. He ran away from his Kentucky home when about twelve years old, was water boy with surveyors in Death Valley, drove or worked on a borax wagon in the twenty-mule-team days, was a rider in Buffalo Bill's wild-west show, and married a New York girl while showing in New York. When the Mispah Ledge at Tonopah started the Goldfield-Tonopah-Ryolite gold rush in 1900, he returned to the region he had known as water boy and mule skinner with confident predictions that he would find gold because of what he had learned in Death Valley and the Panamint Mountains in his boyhood. While in New York he had met Julian Gerard, brother of James W. Gerard and vice-president of the Knickerbocker Trust Company, who grubstaked him to fifteen hundred dollars.

Scott was a great showman. He disappeared into the desert, and nothing was heard of him for some time. Then he appeared at Riverside with a sealed bag, padlocked and bound with chains. He was always smart enough to let others do the questioning. He wasn't very communicative, but confided to some of the questioners that he had twelve thousand dollars' worth of gold amalgam in the bag. Evidently Scotty didn't know too much about mining then, for no mine produces gold amalgam, and there was no stamp mill which could produce anything of that kind in the desert. So canny Riverside, which isn't far from the edge of the Mojave Desert, smiled and didn't get excited.

Scotty kept mum, and nothing was heard of him again till he reported to police in Philadelphia that he had been robbed of his padlocked bag containing

130 pounds of gold amalgam. Philadelphia didn't know amalgam is a mill product, not a mine product, and the story made the wire services, along with Scotty's philosophic remark that there was plenty more dust where that had come from. The stolen bag was never found, but that report relieved Scotty of the necessity of showing it to Gerard.

He went on to New York to get more grubstake money to go back after the "plenty more where that came from." Gerard seems to have been hesitant, but Burden Gaylord, a New York mining engineer, was affected by Scotty's showmanship and advanced him several thousand dollars.

In July, 1905, Scotty rode into the Mojave Desert town of Barstow on a mule and announced he wanted to charter a special train to get to Chicago as quickly as possible. No one had ever chartered a special train from Barstow, though it is almost on the edge of the Calico mining district and is the place where the first borax mining was done. Everyone got excited, and Scotty bought drinks for all. Then he chartered a special train to Los Angeles—despite his great hurry to get to Chicago—and by the time he got there newspaper stories that he had struck it rich in Death Valley had preceded him. Several hundred persons met the train with cheers and followed Scotty from the station to the Hollenbeck Hotel, then the city's best. Still forgetting his great hurry, Scotty received informally in the bar of the Hollenbeck and waited till next day to call on John J. Byrnes, general passenger agent of the Santa Fe west of Albuquerque.

Then Scotty was in a hurry again. He talked as if he would buy the entire Santa Fe system if he had to in order to get to Chicago in forty-six hours which would have been record-breaking time.

On July 9, 1905, the Coyote Special pulled out of Los Angeles. It carried only a small party: Scotty, his wife, Charlie Van Loan—a great newspaperman and short-story writer, Scotty's yellow dog, and a publicity man for the railroad. What there was of the train was as luxurious as could be. Even the menu was a showman's dream:

Caviar sandwiches à la Death Valley
Iced consommé
Porterhouse à la Coyote, two inches thick
Squab on toast, with strips of bacon au Scotty
Ice cream with colored trimmings
Cheese   Coffee   Cigars

Scotty's dash for a speed record was the biggest news of the country. There were throngs at every station through which the special snorted. Wherever it stopped, big crowds gathered and shouted for only a look at Scotty, if they couldn't get a speech. The train had no time to stop at any of the towns in which there were no wire service correspondents, but Charlie Van Loan had handouts for all the newspaper boys, big and little. The whole country panted as Scotty gained minutes and then hours on the schedule. Stations most of the country had never heard of got their names into the newspapers by wiring whether the train had gained or lost a minute since it had left the latest previous station. "The little Arizona towns winked once at the Coyote and were lost in the darkness behind it." The crowds in little New Mexico towns could only shout: "Here she comes, there she goes!" Colorado and Kansas and Missouri forgot everything else to crowd to the stations, no matter at what time of day or night the train was due. Illinois made a holiday of the last day of the trip. And when it was officially announced that Scotty had covered the 2,244½ miles in forty-four hours and forty-four minutes he was the momentary hero of all the land. That was thirteen hours and five minutes faster than the Santa Fe's fastest scheduled limited train, and three hours six minutes faster than the contract called for.

Chicago celebrated. The newspapers overflowed with Scotty. There were stories that he lighted cigars with ten-dollar bills. Thousands of persons were inspired by visions of going west and getting suddenly rich. Scotty's wife confided that the trip cost seventy thousand dollars.

Showman Scotty remained in Chicago only long enough for the publicity to have its fling and went on to New York—as an ordinary passenger on the Twentieth-Century Limited. A New York paper heralded his coming by announcing: "Death Valley Scotty has taken $141,000,000 out of a mine in Death Valley and has spent nearly all. Julian M. Gerard, vice-president of the Knickerbocker Trust Company, once grubstaked Scotty for $4,000. Now that the mine has panned out rich Gerard comes in for a half ownership."

A crowd of about one thousand was at Grand Central Station when Scotty and his yellow dog detrained, and that afternoon he had to hold a levee at his hotel. He began it by ordering four quarts of whisky for the reporters. He explained his yellow dog by saying that when he had been down and out in Los Angeles no one had befriended him, and he had rescued the dog from a crowd that was chasing it with rocks. He said he fed the dog milk out of a silver dish.

But apparently there was no money to divvy with Gerard. When eventually the facts came out it was learned the train had cost Scotty only fifty-five hundred dollars instead of seventy thousand dollars and had been paid for with hundred-dollar bills.

There is no record that Scotty ever cashed in any large amounts of gold dust. In a trial in Los Angeles years later, Scotty testified he had paid for the train out of ten thousand dollars advanced him by a New York mining engineer. No one can estimate the publicity value of the trip to the railroad.

Somewhere during that period Scotty met Albert M. Johnson, president of the National Life Insurance Company of America, a Chicago multimillionaire who was in bad health. Scotty assured him the desert would restore his health and amused him with his fabulous yarns. Johnson could afford to support a jester, and that was virtually what Scotty became. He made good on one thing—the desert did benefit Johnson's health, and the amusement he found in Scotty doubtless helped.

The "$141,000,000" a credulous New York newspaper credited to Scotty seems to have been entirely consumed by that dash across the country, for Scotty next attracted attention, according to Glasscock, as the hero of a melodrama in San Francisco, playing opposite Laurette Taylor in an opus written by Charles A. Taylor. The title was *Scotty, King of the Desert Mine.*

San Francisco knew no mine produced amalgam or hundred-dollar bills and seemed inclined to coldshoulder the production. But then came the Battle of Wingate Pass. Scotty consented to take some doubting Thomases out to see his mine, but in Wingate Pass they were fired on by "bandits," and Scotty's brother, Warner, was wounded seriously. Scotty was the hero of the adventure—and the play opened in San Francisco to packed houses. According to what Johnson confided to Glasscock, the whole thing was a "plant," and the shooting of Warner Scott was, of course, accidental. But it effectively put an end to the expedition to visit Scotty's mine and convinced the country a gang of desperadoes was seeking that mine.

In 1912, Scotty announced he had sold his mine for one million dollars, naming some prominent western men as purchasers. That reminded a Dr. Lawton, who had saved Warner after the accidental shooting, that his bill never had been paid. Dr. Lawton took legal action, for Millionaire Scotty never had been able to pay that bill, and Scotty had to admit to the Los Angeles County Grand Jury that the hole in Death Valley was, according to a newspaper report, "a myth used for years to fill the pockets of promoters." Scotty said he never had said he had a mine but had referred to it as a hole from which he could get all the money he wanted.

But did that convince people Scotty didn't have a wonderful hidden gold mine? Oh, no. They merely thought he was keeping his secret. That confession put Scotty off the front pages for a few years, but in 1924 a Goldfield dispatch reported he was "building on a large scale." In Kansas City in 1929, Scotty told reporters he had lost $6,000,000 in the crash and guessed he would have to fire a couple of hundred employees. It probably was Johnson, if anyone, who had lost the $6,000,000. In the early 1930's the "large scale" building operations, carried on with just enough mystery to provoke inquiry, made newspaper syndicates and national magazines send reporters to see what Scotty was doing in Death Valley, and the rotogravures began to blossom with pictures of his "$150,000 music room," his "$10,000 stable," his "$40,000 bedroom," his "$50,000 guest house," his "$100,000 living room" and his eighteen fireplaces. Scotty confided that his castle was costing $2,300,000.

Then, in 1933, President Roosevelt signed the document that made Death Valley a national monument, and Johnson discovered Scotty had no title to the land on which the castle had been built —with Johnson's money. It took an act of Congress to permit Johnson to buy 1,529 acres, including the castle and grounds, as government land at $1.25 an acre. Senator Pittman of Nevada sponsored the bill, and President Roosevelt signed it, but it expressly provided that all mineral rights in the land remained the property of the United States Government. Speaking for the measure, Senator Pittman said the castle had cost $500,000 but was not yet completed. The Inyo County assessor's records showed that the property was assessed at less than three per cent of the $2,300,000 Scotty grandly asserted "he" had put into it. The property is recorded in the name of A. M. Johnson. Glasscock quotes Johnson as saying:

"I've been paying Scotty's bills for years and I like it. He repays me in laughs."

Yet most of us cherish our illusions with sweet, abiding faith. Thousands of persons annually pay a dollar plus tax to visit Scotty's castle. They rave over the furnishings, the art objects, the $40,000 bedroom in which Scotty has never slept, and those who have caught a glimpse of Scotty, who has a hideout home not far away, are thrilled. You can't fool them—they know anyone who would spend $2,300,000 on a desert home must have found one of California's great lost mines, no matter what skeptics say. They want to believe the Scotty legend, just as they want to believe that the swallows always return to Capistrano Mission on St. John's Day, though often the swallows are days off schedule. Like the La Jollans, the Azusans, the people who make heroes of Murrietta and Vazquez, and those who seek the magic waters of El Polin, they love the old tradition and defend it. In many cases the Californians have been told what they believe by their fathers or grandfathers or great-grandfathers, and surely anything handed down that way is far more correct than any of the theories of mere foolish students of history.

TO THROW DIGNITY OUT THE WINDOW

THE Spanish settlers of California were inherently people of dignity and ceremony. They liked to do things with an air. But they also loved dancing and fiestas and seemed to feel that a certain amount of austerity earned them the right to take their hair down, literally. In fiesta seasons the girls wore their hair loose, so they could shake the *cascarones* out of it. Instead of three days of carnival before Lent, they enjoyed two weeks of festivities to put themselves in a proper state of penitence. When Good Friday came they would make a celebration of hanging Judas in effigy. When Easter was past, the elders, who had refrained from chastising children during the holy season of restraint and forgiveness, got out their switches and evened up a few cherished scores. And Christmas was a two-week festival, in which even some of the religious observances became more exuberant than dignified.

La Noche Buena, or Christmas Eve, was always marked by the drama of *"Los Pastores,"* or "The Shepherds," which still may be seen in many communities in California. In *Mission Tales* Mrs. Forbes describes one Christmas Eve in Santa Clara Mission in the good old days. Practically every one from the near-by pueblo of San Jose was in the gay procession of horsemen and *caretas* which paraded to the mission for the event. The men riders wore jackets of velvet embroidered in silver and gold, snug-fitting trousers widened by slashings between the knee and the ankle, the edges caught by silver buckles, or knee breeches and embroidered leggings with tasseled garters. The women were dressed less showily unless they were in a wedding party, of which there were always several. The saddles were of finest tooled leather, mounted with silver and often embroidered with

gold or silver. Most of the women rode in front of
the men.

When they reached the mission, all the benches
were cleared from the floor so that the drama
might be presented on it, and the spectators lined
the walls all around. Then distant singing was
heard, and the tinkling of guitars within the chapel
signaled the approach of the procession.

"Heading the procession were the shepherds and
singers," writes Mrs. Forbes, "followed by the
Archangel Michael, Lucifer, a character representing Satan, and a lazy, clownish fellow named Bartolo. Having passed several times around the
church, the singers retired to the choir loft and the
play began. The whole story was told in song, with
very little acting. When the angel announced the
birth of Christ and led the shepherds to the manger
a deep reverential spell settled over the audience.

"The appearance of Satan at this critical moment, with his sarcasm and discordant gibes, jarred
on the listeners. The conflicting influences exerted
on the shepherds by the angel and Satan were soon
reflected on the audience. The godly and religious
applauded the angel and encouraged him to further efforts while the boys and the rabble hugely
enjoyed the part taken by Satan. His horns and
tail and cloven feet were commented on and
snatched at by the more daring. The one lazy,

good-for-nothing shepherd, Bartolo, lay on his sheepskin, shouting rude personal jokes at the audience, convulsing the rougher element and fascinating the boys."

The victory of good over evil was loudly cheered, and when Bartolo took up his dirty sheepskin and slunk out "the better element was much relieved." The next act was the manger scene, wholly reverential, but after that came a scene in which the angel and Satan engaged in violent physical combat which looked nip and tuck for a while. When at last the evil one was worsted, "to cover his discomfiture he rushed at a wild-eyed, scared-looking Indian and chased him down the Alameda till he tripped and fell, and the Devil smote him with the flat of his sword, completely terrifying the Indian."

A previous chapter told of the battles with *cascarones*, the egg shells filled with brightly colored bits of tinsel or perfume which were crushed on the heads of others at even many of the most dignified parties and celebrations. Another feature of the Christmas celebration was the smashing of a huge bag filled with all sorts of sweets and prizes. The bag was hung high, and a man with a club would smite it so that as it burst the contents flew in all directions, and a mad scramble ensued.

When the Americans roared into California they developed their own brands of pomp and ceremony

—and buffoonery. In the mining camps, men's love of ritual found expression in lodges. Every important ghost town in the West has its lodge hall or two, for lodges and volunteer fire departments became the exclusive clubs in communities which had no other social gauges. One may wonder why it is that, in a land which always has boasted its democracy, you can't bring a group of fifty together in the wilderness without having someone try to start an exclusive set in it. The lodges of the mining camps went in for pomp in the biggest way possible. The volunteer fire department looked on themselves as their communities' heroes. And the ribald crew who couldn't get into either formed chapters of E. Clampus Vitus.

E. Clampus Vitus had a ritual more dignified than any of the others, in that it bristled with real Latin and imitation Latin. It announced itself as an organization for the benefit of widows and orphans—especially widows. Its patron saint was St. Vitus. Its chief was the Noble Grand Humbug. When a tenderfoot in a mining camp yearned to get into one of the exclusive secret orders, E. Clampus Vitus took him in, and how! It put him through a ritual which made him tremble and often through an initiation full of physical hardship. And then it was revealed it was all a hoax—

and in those days the victim of a hoax of that kind was expected to buy drinks for all the hoaxers.

In many historic spots in California today you find bronze markers put there by E. Clampus Vitus. It has done a great deal to unearth and preserve authentic history. Its members now are mainly historians, college professors, members of San Francisco's famous Pioneer Society, which was organized less than three years after San Francisco ceased to be Yerba Buena, scholars on the staffs of the Bancroft Library and the Huntington Library, and descendants of pioneers. It has done many serious and fine things, but it has done them all without a trace of dignity. Its meetings are boisterously convivial. Its proceedings are a succession of jokes and hoaxes, often ribald. Yet it has made pilgrimages to nearly every historic spot in California, including many at which the pilgrims had to sleep on the ground in sleeping bags and cook their meals over camp fires. And it has taught them the history of those places as perhaps no other historical organization has. And maybe that is more in the California tradition than any more dignified plan of operations could be.

Perhaps nothing else illustrates so well as does the Pioneer Society of San Francisco how quickly people became "old settlers" in California. The Pioneer Society was organized in 1850, and at first excluded all persons who hadn't been in California in 1849. The one year since '49 had brought California more changes than many areas have seen in a century. That society has been invaluable to California, for, but for the pioneers, many historical records would have been lost in those years when changes came too swiftly for most persons to count or remember; yet many of its members have never let their respect for rare records and rare books exceed their respect for rare vintages, and among their most honored ancestors are those who invented a mellow but convincing drink known as Pisco Punch.

San Franciscans do not hesitate to assure you their Bohemian Club is the most famous club "in the world." It was founded by a few journalists in 1872 and had only twenty charter members. Its constitution limited membership to "gentlemen professionally connected with music, art and the drama and those who, by reason of love and appreciation of those subjects, may be deemed eligible." That latter loophole allowed many wealthy men to come in and carry the financial burden, and today the Bohemian Club not only has commodious and luxurious quarters in San Francisco but a magnificent grove of virgin redwoods on the Russian River, which was named for the Russians who settled in that region in 1811. There many of

the members have luxurious "cabins"—with but-
lers and all that sort of thing—and there the club
holds its annual Hi-Jinks.

It seems safe to say that those events annually
attract more celebrities from greater distances than
do any other social events annually held. Famous
editors, actors, writers, musicians, and artists leave
their work in New York, Boston, Miami, and many
intermediate points to attend the Hi-Jinks, and often there are noted visitors from other countries.
The doings, which are for men only, are supposed
to be secret, but they may open with a torchlight
procession, headed by a band playing the Dead
March, and the burial of Care, the obsequies being
honored by a rousing wake. It is against the law
for anyone to dig up Care again for the duration of
the outing, or at least two weeks.

Many of the country's brightest minds are kept
busy thinking up frolics and surprises for every
day, and the windup is a theatrical performance on
which no money or pains have been spared. On at
least one occasion the San Francisco Symphony Orchestra was taken out to play for that production.
They say that no other amateur productions anywhere are so lavishly staged, costumed, and
equipped. Of course, they are far from being wholly
amateur, for many famous folk take part in them,
but the interesting thing is that financiers, indus-

trialists, and even politicians, who all their lives have dreamed of artistic expression but have turned to more lucrative efforts, often find their chance at last in those performances and throw themselves into them with enthusiasm and devotion. A few years ago an operetta written by a capitalist and scored by an attorney for the Bohemian Grove Hi-Jinks was successfully reproduced in Monte Carlo by a producer who had been impressed by it at the Grove. Once I was talking with a friend who for twenty years had been a notably successful motion-picture writer and was then drawing a salary of fifteen hundred dollars a week. He had written all or part of more than a hundred pictures which had been shown all over the world. I asked:

"Of all the things you have written, which is the one you love the best?"

He stared a moment, then opened a desk drawer and drew out a battered paper-backed volume. It was a play he had written for the Hi-Jinks while he was a young newspaper man in San Francisco.

"I'm prouder of this than of anything else I ever wrote," he said, "because I put my whole untrammeled heart into it. I didn't get a cent for it, but they had a few copies printed to show their appreciation."

At the Grove they bury Care and throw dignity out the window for two weeks, even when dealing with ex-Presidents and dignitaries. But when the "jinks" are over they often have to revive Care because of headaches. San Franciscans boast that their Olympic Club, founded in 1860, is the father of all the great athletics and sports clubs in the world. They are fond of their Family Club, started as a sort of balance to the Bohemians. But San Francisco is essentially a bohemian city and looks on the Bohemian Club as a true expression of its spirit.

The perpetuation of old traditions is the main reason for organizing groups in California. Nearly every community has its historical society, besides which there are county and state historical societies. Then there are History and Landmarks clubs, Roads to Romance associations, Mission Trails association, Native Sons of the Golden West, Native Daughters of the Golden West, groups specially interested in preserving memories of the Gold Rush, of steamboating, of ranching, of Arabian and Palomino horse breeding in California. The Zamorano Club of Los Angeles is made up mainly of art printers who specialize in California history. The Wells Fargo Bank in San Francisco maintains a museum and a library which specialize in the history of the Gold Rush, and the Pioneer Society also has a library which is a godsend to researchers. So does the Southwest Museum in Los Angeles.

Driving through California, you may come on

several towns in which all the men are raising
beards for their own community's centennial celebration or an annual Pioneer Days picnic. In Los
Angeles you may see men and women in the costumes of a century ago casually shopping or walking unconcernedly along crowded sidewalks. They
are not self-conscious, for they have often dressed
that way for affairs in the leading hotels or in
Olvera Street, a little street which has been turned
into a Mexican market place, in the midst of which
is the old adobe house commandeered by Stockton
and Frémont when Los Angeles was captured in
1846. Those men and women are on the way to
a meeting of Los Fiesteros de Los Angeles, and at
those parties, held at least once a month, heirloom
costumes are much in evidence. Rarely is there a
solemn note when Los Fiesteros meet. They love to
toss dignity in a blanket.

Los Rancheros Visitadores of Santa Barbara isn't
an old organization but has become so famous that
every year many east-coast horsemen and sports-
men ship their horses by air to take part in its annual pilgrimages. It was in 1929 that Ed Borein,
noted Western artist, suggested that "a few of the
boys" have an old-fashioned outing in his chuck
wagon. That same year John Mitchell and his wife,
the former Lolita Armour, both from Chicago,
bought a ranch near Santa Barbara and went West-

ern in a big way. They named the ranch Rancho
Juan y Lolita. Mitchell got Elmer Awl, who knew
more of such things than he did, to dash about
through California buying up old stagecoaches,
pioneer wagons, antique saddles, and other accou-
trements that would give the ranch an atmosphere
of bygone days. These he had repaired by experts
and polished like jewels. In brief, with true Chicago
enterprise, he evoked the days of the dons as most
of us evoke memories of childhood—with all their
radiance and none of their discomfort. He surrounded himself with heirloom stuff and became
Don Juan, a valiant knight in defense of the old
tradition in a community which glorifies its traditions.

The next year sixty-five men met at Rancho Juan
y Lolita. Mitchell had only adopted the custom of
the country when he became "donny" with enthusiasm. Don T. Wilson Dibblee, Don Dwight Murphy, and various millionaires from far and near,
who had acquired country estates on which they
raised pedigreed horses or cattle, had been taking
part in Santa Barbara fiestas for years and often
actually felt as Spanish as they looked when dressed
for their parts. It was Dibblee who gave the group
its name of Los Rancheros Visitadores. The aims of
the organization were to revive the custom of Spanish days, when the rancheros moved from ranch to

ranch for the spring roundup or rodeo, and to have a good time. Don Dwight Murphy invited them all to come to his ranch the next month as his guests, for a rodeo with comedy relief and plenty of refreshments. The rule was that costumes of fifty years or more before should be worn. No automobiles were permitted. There were three stagecoaches and a covered wagon for any who did not wish to make the trip on horseback, but nearly everyone went horseback. The invitations said that plenty of cards and poker chips would be provided, the affair would be strictly stag, and each guest was expected to bring his own LINIMENT.

Ninety men made the first Visitadores trip. Now the annual cavalcade numbers about five hundred. Among the riders are men who have spent fortunes trying to standardize the complexions of Palomino horses, who have barns finer than the homes most persons live in and tack rooms in which one may see fifty thousand dollars' worth of silver saddles alone. There are beautiful horses and beautiful costumes and vehicles which make you rub your eyes, feeling they should be in museums instead of on the highway. But those men ride thirty miles a day for at least four days, and most of them do it on horseback. Each night they camp at a different ranch, and though they rough it de luxe, it is a test of endurance for many of the riders. Some of the eastern horses, wholly unused to such broad open spaces and such lengthy journeys, find it more than they can endure.

Besides the thirty-mile stints, there is much riding up and down the line of march and plenty of horseplay—not by horses—in that gay cavalcade. Where they pitch camp there are plenty of employees to do the hard work, and chefs—and bartenders. Their apparel may proclaim the men to be Spanish caballeros, southwestern cowboys, pioneer Americans, or dazzling men who learned to ride and shoot in military academies and never saw a real ranch till, as Hollywood movie stars, they went to one on location. But when they camp they are likely to have impromptu rodeos and frolics, much as did the early-day rancheros they imitate, and sometimes the excitement grows intense. On one occasion vague hints were dropped that they were near a reservation full of Indians, who sometimes got bad when they were full of liquor. At the proper moment a band of braves in full war dress rushed out on the encampment, brandishing knives and apparently bent on scalping all the whites. One brave seized one of the guests by the hair and deftly scalped him, to the horror of not only the spectators but also the scalper and the scalpee, for many had partaken of more or less bottled cheer and the scalp came off as clean as a whistle. It was

a minute before anyone realized it was only a tou-
pee.

That gives a vague idea of the way Los Rancheros
Visitadores carry on the old tradition and preserve
history. The Murphys and Mitchells and Dibblees
and many others, even some who have come from
other states in recent years, feel they are perpetuat-
ing something which came to them with the land
they have bought, and, because of their prosperity
and their competition for antiques which will help
create the atmosphere they want, they have helped
make a great part of rural Santa Barbara County
a place of beautiful ranches, magnificent horses,
and much that is of true historic interest. They get
to know their back country and its history and folklore almost as well as did the real dons who used
to own those lands. And after they have taken
part in half a dozen Visitadores pilgrimages and as
many Santa Barbara fiestas, dressing and riding
and looking the part and reviving old practices on
their ranches, blessed if they don't seem to feel they
are real dons.

The De Anza Riders, organized at Riverside, is a
similar organization. In midwinter it makes its annual pilgrimage over a hundred miles or so of the
mountains and desert De Anza conquered at that
season. The difference is that now there are well-
marked roads—cleared by snowplows if necessary

—and easy grades, and they not only know where they are going but are sure they will be entertained when they get there. Their only pitfall is that in some cases their hosts may be the wily subdividers of new desert townsites, something the Visitadores have sedulously avoided. But, like the Visitadores, the motivating idea behind the Riders was a desire to bring back the old tradition and make it a part of modern life—and to do it in an area in which every man should carry along a little snakebite remedy for his own or his friends' protection.

All through California you find groups doing worthy things in a gay and often slapstick manner rather than with what in other lands would be considered befitting dignity. The breakfast-club idea, now virulent in many parts of the country, originated in Los Angeles. A group of men who used to ride horseback in Griffith Park before going to their daily occupations formed the club so they could breakfast together when they returned from their ride. For that purpose they acquired a few acres of ground, built a clubhouse in which several hundred persons could breakfast—or dine or dance if that suited them better—and soon had hundreds at their weekly breakfasts. Everyone at them had to put his arms around the shoulders of the men on each side of him and roar out a parody on the song "Tammany" which began, "Ham and eggs, ham and eggs." The breakfast-club idea swept Los Angeles like a grass fire in August. The original group breakfasted at eight, but soon there were others which breakfasted at nine, at ten, at noon. There were women's, blind persons', hard-of-hearing persons', teachers' breakfast clubs. Any church, lodge or group was likely to organize a breakfast club.

Herbert Hoover, visiting Los Angeles at that time, sighed: "It's a good city but it has one terrible vice. It's the only place on earth where they make speeches at breakfast." But no criticism prevailed against the breakfast-club idea. It spread to other cities, other states, and in many it may have lost its original California flavor. If so, let it be recalled that the big idea of California's most famous social organizations is to do something worth doing—but to throw dignity out the window and do it in an exuberant and devil-may-care way.

TO DRESS DRAMATICALLY

WHEN Portolá marched north from San Diego in 1769, "with that small company of persons, or, rather, say skeletons, who had been spared by scurvy, hunger and thirst," as his own words described them, they still affected a certain jauntiness. They wore sleeveless leather jackets and on their left arms carried bullhide shields with which to protect both themselves and their horses from arrows. The horses wore a kind of armor, too, a sort of skirt of leather hung from the saddle to protect the thighs and legs from thorns and brush. The soldiers carried lances, broadswords, and short muskets. Each soldier had six horses for remounts and a colt and a mule, and one horse was kept saddled, day and night. And, despite scurvy, hunger, and thirst, they must have cut quite a dash, for Miguel Coscanso, who accompanied the expedition as engineer, wrote: "It is not too much to say they are the best horsemen in the world." So far as is known, that was the first time anyone claimed that something in California was "the best in the world."

The California male animal has always been something of a peacock, inclined to dress a little more dramatically and showily than most men. The early Californian wore a gay blue jacket trimmed with bright red cuffs and collar, and blue pantaloons buttoned down the side but slit at the knee to show the white stocking underneath. His deerskin leggings were handsomely embroidered, and his head was covered with a broadbrimmed flat-crowned sombrero, under which his black hair hung braided in a queue. His serape could serve as blanket for man or horse, as cape or overcoat, and it was always gay.

Horses were so important in the lives of the early settlers that a rider practically looked on their trappings as part of his own costume. The saddle was a huge affair and was laid on a broad apron of leather, stamped and embroidered in red, green, gold, and silver. The bridle of braided horsehair was silver mounted. The stirrups had long leather coverings in front. The spurs were cruel, but were inlaid with silver.

Though the men were the peacocks, an early Spanish governor, making requisitions for settlers, demanded plenty of ribbons and furbelows for the ladies, declaring he didn't want settlers who wouldn't dress up. Brigida Briones, writing in 1827, said: "Ladies were rarely seen on the streets except in early morning on the way to mass. They went attended by servants who carried small mats to kneel on, as there were no seats, and the church floors were hard, cold and damp. Their dress was very plain, a black rebozo on head and shoulders, a black petticoat. . . . For home wear and company the well to do had silks, laces and velvet. There was much rivalry of dress among the beauties and those of small means often underwent privations in order to equal the rich."

That sounds as if the girls did pretty well at home or at parties, but the everyday garb in which the men went about was "a broadbrimmed hat of dark color, a gilt or figured band around the crown, lined under the rim with silk, a short silk or velvet jacket, a shirt open at the neck, pantaloons open at the sides below the knee, usually of velveteen or broadcloth and gilt laced, deerskin shoes, dark brown and much ornamented, a red sash around the waist and poncho or serape. The latter was always a mark of the rank of the owner and was of black or dark blue broadcloth with velvet trimmings," and in many cases the trimmings made it both gay and rich.

Richard Henry Dana was present at the marriage of Alfred Robinson, a young New Englander, to Ana Maria de la Alta Gracia Leonora, one of the daughters of Captain José Antonio de la Guerra y Moriega, at Santa Barbara. As Robinson was agent for the ships in the hide and tallow trade, Dana's ship was decked with flags. At ten o'clock the bride, dressed in black, was seen with her sister on the way to confessional. An hour later the great doors of the mission church swung open, the bells pealed, the ship fired a salute of twenty-three guns, and the bride, now robed in white, emerged with the bridegroom. The sailors were given shore leave to attend a fandango at the home of the bride's parents, where a large tent had been erected, and all were expected to come without invitation. All the inhabitants of the town, men, women, and children, who could get there were present. "The costumes of our sailors were much admired," writes

Dana. "Our agent, in a tight black swallow tailed coat just imported from Boston, and high stiff cravat, looked as if he had been pinned and skewered, with only his feet and hands left free."

Possibly had Dana seen Robinson so attired in Boston he would have regarded him with admiration, but his contrast with the more colorful and far more comfortable garb of the California man was too great. Above the knee, the Californians' trousers fitted with the snugness of riding breeches, because all of them rode, but otherwise they were comfortable, graceful, and colorful.

W. W. Robinson, present-day authority on California history, is not a descendant of Alfred Robinson, who arrived in California in 1827. In that period, according to Dana, the women wore gowns of silk, crepe, calico, or any other material the ships brought in, with short sleeves, loose waists, no corsets, shoes of kid or satin, sashes or belts of bright colors, and almost always earrings and necklaces. They had no bonnets, and if they were unmarried their hair hung loose or in long braids. Married women wore their hair done up on a high comb, and it would be hard for any woman not to look rather dashing with her hair done up on a high comb. Over the head the mantilla was thrown, and when the wearer was out of doors it was drawn close about the face. In their homes the women wore small scarves or neckerchiefs and about their heads a band with a star or ornament in front.

But compare the bridegroom Dana described to one married in Los Angeles in 1842, as described by Mrs. Sanchez:

"Yellow hat of vicuna wool, with a heavy string of glass beads around the crown, the under part of the brim neatly covered with silver lace. The jacket easy fitting, of green satin, with large flaps of the same material, the buttons being made of Mexican pesetas, with the eagle stamp on the outside. The waistcoat was of yellow satin with the pocket flaps buttoned up with gold dollars. Wide breeches of red velvet to the knees, where they were fastened with silver buckles. A deerskin legging of the natural color, tied around the knee where the breeches ended with green silk ribbon making a flower, and with tassels from which depended little figures of cats, dogs, puppets, etc. made of seed-glass beads, interspersed with gold and silver thread. The serape was of sky-blue cloth of finest quality, the opening for the head faced with black velvet and edged all around with fringed silver galloon. Where the deerskin leggings ended began the shoes, sharp pointed and turned upward. The long hair, braided in a queue, hung down upon the jacket, where the queue was tied with a large flower of green ribbon. To light his cigarette he used a *mechero* [steel and flint case] from which hung an ornament of beads, beautifully made. The tinder was perfumed with Peruvian balsam."

Presumably the bride was just dressed in conventional white.

That bridegroom was a very rich young man. Here is a truer account of marriage customs in general:

"When the marriage contract is agreed upon, it is the first care of the bridegroom to get, by buying, begging or stealing, the finest horse possible and also a saddle and silver mounted bridle. The over-leathers of the saddle must also be embroidered. These articles are indispensable, no matter how poor the parties might be. The bridegroom must furnish the bride with at least six articles of each kind of women's clothing and everything necessary to feast the wedding guests for one, two or three days. On the wedding day the bridegroom takes up before him on his horse the future godmother, and the future godfather takes the bride before him on another fine horse, and so they gallop to church. The ceremony over, the newly-married couple mount one horse, the future godparents the other, and so they gallop back to the house of the bride's parents, where they are received with tears and blessings and a salute of rockets and muskets."

Early American settlers rather fancied the Spanish and Mexican modes, had their trousers cut the same way, and blossomed out in blue jackets and sombreros. The American gamblers took to the native costumes, too, but modified them to show shiny starched shirt fronts with diamond solitaire studs. They also preferred high hats to the low-crowned sombrero. And the miners felt they were properly dressed in red shirts and high boots. One early American governor was a dandy in buff trousers and vest, blue coat with shiny brass buttons, and ruffled shirt.

The alacrity with which Americans adopted Spanish freedom and daring in the matter of dress is suggested by the fact that the *London Illustrated News* in 1850 found San Francisco's celebration of the admission of California as a state worth reporting in both words and pictures. The chief marshal of the celebration parade was in white and gold, his guards in sky blue and silver. The mayor and aldermen wore dark blue scarves with gold trimmings and white armlets. The aristocratic volunteer firemen wore red shirts. The Chinese were gorgeous in lavender trousers and plum-colored jackets of silk. The Spanish caballeros wore ranchero costumes with crimson and green boleros. Though San Francisco had been San Francisco and part of the United States only three years, it had its National Guard, cadet, zouave, grenadier, hussar, and dragoon companies, all dazzlingly attired, and the Irish battalion in towering shakos, the schutzen-verein, the Hibernians all in green, the Germania Rifles, the Garibaldi Guards, and the Guardia de Juarez all had done their best to appear in distinctive and outstanding uniforms.

From San Francisco to Virginia City, the volunteer fire departments in the Gold Rush towns became social organizations of distinction. When they gave a ball or paraded they were in full regalia, each trying to outshine and outglow the others in costumes and in splendor. Even in San Francisco they included many of the most prominent citizens, for San Francisco was swept by six devastating fires in its first few years—fires which would have wiped any less spirited town off the map. Membership in any of the volunteer fire companies was a badge of honor, labeling one as a defender of the city.

Though the vaqueros were rather jaunty-looking fellows, the first American cowboys weren't. The original American cowboys wore jeans and shirtsleeves and usually vests, because vest pockets were handy for tobacco and cigarette papers. They tied hides around their legs to protect them while riding through thorny brush and tied large handkerchiefs around their necks, letting them hang down in front, so that when milling cattle kicked up a lot of dust they could hold the handkerchiefs over their noses. According to Ken Maynard, who was a rider with Buffalo Bill, that clever showman got theatrical costume designers to invent the cowboy costume now affected on all the dude ranches. The hides became chaps, the neckerchief a gay thing gracefully hanging down the back. The vest vanished or was replaced by a gay bolero. Thus was the spirit of the West affected by Broadway.

In recent years the fast-growing clothing industry in California has been inspired by the state's innumerable costumed pageants, by Californians' love of the out of doors, and by the numerous famous designers in the motion-picture studios. They began by making garments for actors, who love to attract attention, and then timidly tempted the market with sports clothes which would have been considered fantastic and utterly undignified a quarter of a century ago. Now they appeal so to the public that it is not unusual to see large advertisements in New York, Boston, Miami, and midwestern newspapers announcing "latest Hollywood sports styles."

All of them are gay and some are gaudy, but to a certain extent they are setting American men free from the ruts of conventional dress in which they have been channeled for some generations. Unquestionably the clothes a man wears and sees about him affect his actions and feelings and even his character. A circus wouldn't be any fun if the clown were dressed like an undertaker. The traditional fear men have of being dressed conspicuously—that is, differently from all the other men around them—is being dispelled. And maybe it is California's love of the dramatic and the romantic in dress that is helping to do it.

IN EVERY American state the pioneers have had to conquer the seemingly impossible, but those who blazed the trails to California had to overcome the greatest hardships of them all. It was a longer and more hazardous trip across the plains, the deserts, and the mountains, or around the Horn, than it was across the ocean from Europe, and when the settlers got to California those same barriers stood between them and anyone who could

[276]

comfort or succor them. The first adventurers overland aroused the fears of many fierce tribes of Indians who knew how to use flood and famine, Donner Pass and Death Valley, as their allies. In the
guise of friends, they could mislead or misdirect
the wagon trains into ambush, flood, or waterless
desert in which horses and cattle and people died
till the trails were marked with skeletons.

Thus it became a California custom to tackle
problems never met before and devise new ways of
doing things.

The idea that the California Indians were a sub-
missive and rather inferior lot is not correct. It was
not till 1873 that the United States Army finally
conquered the Indians of the High Sierra, and there
had been many a massacre before that. In 1775,
eight hundred Indians attacked San Diego Mission,
beat Father Luis Jaume to death, killed a carpenter
and wounded six more men, and set fire to the
church. Nearly every other mission and settlement
had its troubles with the Indians. Nearly a century
later, in 1872, the Modoc Indians massacred an
emigrant train, raided numerous settlers, and defeated a company of soldiers and volunteers who
sought to arrest them. That was the beginning of
the Modoc War. General E. R. S. Canby, commanding forces far outnumbering the Indians, met de-
feat and bafflement. Numerous efforts to conclude

peace failed, the last of them resulting in the murder of General Canby and the Rev. Eleazer Thomas, two of the conferees representing the government, and the wounding of a third. That shocked the distant Army heads into determined action, more troops were sent, and the Indians were surrounded and overwhelmed. Their leader, known as Captain Jack, and his lieutenants were brought to court martial, and on October 2, 1873, were hanged at Fort Klamath. Six Indians in all were hanged and 153 exiled to the Indian Territory.

Indians who could put up such a fight after a hundred years of white domination were a fearsome and dangerous hazard, and every pack train or wagon train from Mexico or from the Missouri River might expect to meet them anywhere in a meandering march of well over a thousand miles. Yet the pioneers dreaded the desert and the mountain passes more. In battle they had a fighting chance. If a wagon broke down in the desert, they had to manufacture parts without tools or materials. If horses or oxen died in the desert, they had to overload other wagons or abandon the necessities of life. If illness came, they were months away from a doctor. Grizzlies, wolves, coyotes, rattlesnakes lay in wait for them in the strange wilderness. Water which looked all right made them ill. Nature, man, and beast opposed them with obstacles they had not ever met before, and they had to gain the know-how of dealing with them as they went along.

So it became a California custom to overrule nature.

Hanna's assertion that no coward dared to start for California in the Gold Rush days and no weakling ever got there was equally true of all the other adventurers and pioneers for three hundred years. They had to tackle the seemingly impossible as a matter of almost daily necessity. And by turning the impossible into the possible they gained a swaggering confidence that has become the heritage of Californians.

They feel that whatever must be done to assure their future can be done and set about doing it with a daring that often startles and even amuses the rest of the country, but that often sets an example and opens up new avenues of progress.

When Los Angeles was only a pueblo, nature provided enough water for its needs. When it grew to be a town of ten thousand it began to realize it was the metropolis of a desert. Agriculture was supplanting sheep and cattle raising on the ranches. Back in the mountains there were springs and streams, but the ranchers used much of that water and what got by them vanished into the sand. The little streams became dust bowls in summer, and the Los Angeles River, the biggest stream, dwindled to a trickle a good horse could leap. During the drought of the 1860's, thousands of wild horses were driven into the sea to save the grass for the cattle, and still the cattle died by tens of thousands. That convinced many persons who tried to be guided by reason that southern California had become overpopulated and would revert to desert for lack of water, and that they had better sell out and go elsewhere.

Nevertheless, the optimists kept on talking of the future, and the people kept coming. On every street corner worriers proved by logic that it couldn't last. Man might overcome nature for a while, but nature always won in the end. When the city reached the hundred-thousand mark in 1900, they shook their heads and sighed that it wouldn't be long now.

But 250 miles away was the Owens Valley and the Owens River, fed by the eternal snows of Mount Whitney and hundreds of other mighty peaks. The Owens Valley was in Inyo and Mono counties, not in Los Angeles County. It was a place of prosperous ranches, and the ranchers wouldn't sell their water to Los Angeles. It took acts of Congress, a bitter war between Los Angeles and the Owens Valley ranchers, and a bond issue the headshakers said would burden the city so it never could survive it, but eventually the city bought the valley by condemnation and a great aqueduct brought the Owens River over range after range of mountains to the city's door.

That was all right till the city reached the million mark and southern California was populated by other millions. Then the city reached out four hundred miles to the Colorado River, the American Nile. The Colorado River drains seven states and empties into the Gulf of California in Mexico. When snows from two hundred to fifteen hundred miles from its mouth melted, it became the red menace of the Colorado Desert, most of which is lower than sea level. "Colorado" is a Spanish word for "red." The millions of tons of silt the river annually carried down raised its bed till it was higher than much of the desert flanking it on both sides, though it flowed between banks of silt of its own making. When the big floods came they burst through those banks and spread over the desert. In 1904, one Charles R. Lockwood, seeking to irrigate desert lands, opened a gap in the river wall, and the flood burst through it, flooding four hundred square miles and forming the Salton Sea. It took over two years for engineers to close that gap.

It called for treaties with seven states and one foreign country, the building of the tallest dam in the world, the building of the greatest hydro-electric plant up to that time, and the boring of a tunnel through Mount San Jacinto, the eleven thousand-foot peak of which had made De Anza and many who came after him groan and almost give up, before southern California could get that water and power for Los Angeles and for many other cities and agricultural areas of California, Arizona, and Nevada, without which their part in production for World War II would have been impossible. Now floods along the Colorado River appear to be things of the past. Nature has been changed from man's enemy to his ally. In a lonely farmhouse in the arid desert you can turn on a faucet and get water which nature bestowed on the earth a thousand miles away, or press a button and get electric current.

There still are head-shakers who say that you can't fool nature all the time, and that eventually Los Angeles will revert to desert. But Los Angeles is already inquiring into the possibility of diverting water from the Columbia River, and when outsiders gasp at such an idea Angelenos calmly add that they might, if necessary, go over to the Mississippi and cure it of the flood habit, while doing themselves a good turn. Already they are piping in natural gas from Texas. With the aid of the Navy, they and the Long Beachites have created one of the greatest harbors in the world where nature never intended a harbor to be. They have come to the conviction that anything called impossible is merely something to which men of imagination have not yet given their efforts.

San Francisco has been even more dramatic. The Golden Gate Bridge and the Bay Bridge might be called the most heroic expression of the California spirit. They were impossible, but they had to be built for the unbottling of San Francisco and the progress of California.

The Golden Gate is a narrow passage connecting the Pacific Ocean and San Francisco, San Pablo, and Suisun bays, which really form one inland sea. That inland sea has a shore line so long that a person in Marin County might be within a mile of San Francisco by airline and yet, to reach it by land, have to travel several hundred miles. If you will form a letter C with the forefinger and thumb of your right hand, the tip of the forefinger will be comparable to the situation of Marin County, and the tip of the thumb to San Francisco. The people of Marin, Sonoma, Mendocino, Napa, and Del Norte counties would be brought vastly closer to San Francisco by a bridge across the Golden Gate, and San Franciscans yearned for suburban homes in the area across that narrow channel.

The Golden Gate Bridge was "impossible" because there would have to be a span of more than

[283]

a mile. A suspension bridge of that length was considered out of the question, and if pillars could be set in the stream the mighty tides would undermine them. For years the Army opposed the building of the bridge on the ground that it would have to be of such enormous bulk it would cork the entire inland sea if it should crumble or be knocked down.

However, San Francisco refused to give up. It had a survey made and discovered that, twelve hundred feet off shore from the south side of the gate, in the open sea, there was a mass of solid rock capable of supporting a greater bridge than man had ever attempted to build. That meant that a suspension bridge could be built with a span only four thousand, two hundred feet long instead of more than a mile long. But still all the conservative people, of whom even San Francisco has a few, shook their heads. The famous Brooklyn Bridge was only one thousand, six hundred feet long, and a suspension bridge more than two and one-half times that long looked like a dangerous experiment.

The engineers who built the bridge had no precedents to go by. The Golden Gate is about a mile wide and three miles long. No light from the sun can penetrate the ocean to a depth of one hundred feet, and the water in the Golden Gate is two hundred feet deep or deeper most of the way. The great mass of solid rock discovered twelve hundred feet off shore was one hundred feet below the surface, and the "impossible" problem was to build, in total darkness that far under water, safe foundations for a tower capable of holding up such a bridge.

Each tower of that bridge had to be strong enough to stand a pull of 63,000,000 pounds from the cables. The towers would have to rise 746 feet above the water, but the one on the San Francisco side would have to rise 846 feet from bedrock, or from 100 feet below the surface of the water. The Eiffel Tower is taller, but it isn't based 100 feet below the surface of the open sea, where it often gets mighty rough.

More than an acre of the ocean floor had to be cleared for the foundations for that tower, which is 250 feet taller than the towers of the George Washington Bridge across the Hudson, the second largest suspension bridge. Deep-sea divers had to go down where there was no light and direct those working above by telephone. Thousands of tons of rock had to be removed to make a place for the foundation. That rock was carried farther out to sea to make a breakwater to modify the breakers, which were twenty feet high at that point.

The effects of heat and cold, of winds and tides and of possible earthquake shocks, had to be allowed for. A fierce wind blowing through the channel may make the towers sway as much as twenty feet, but the highest wind ever recorded there is sixty miles an hour, and the bridge is twice as safe as it would have to be to stand a wind of ninety miles an hour.

This suggests an aside about the old San Francisco custom of speaking of "the fire" instead of "the earthquake." California has had many earthquakes which did great damage, but it is a fact that no Class-A building was ever dangerously damaged by one. Buildings of unreinforced stone or brick have toppled, and even Class-A buildings have shown cracks after a quake, and the plate glass windows in many have popped like firecrackers, but that was all. Well-constructed frame dwellings have been shaken and wrenched but have not collapsed. The San Francisco quake of 1906 started many fires, and the fires swept the city. Today San Francisco shows its disdain of earth shock by building many skyscrapers on which there is no earthquake insurance. It is considered quite unnecessary on Class-A construction.

Today no one fears to cross the Golden Gate Bridge, which stands 220 feet above high tide, its enormous cables hanging like inverted rainbows from the mighty towers, a silver veil across the Golden Gate. Its six lanes of traffic are crowded with motor vehicles, and there are sidewalks for foot passengers. The full length of the bridge is 8,940 feet.

The Bay Bridge, connecting San Francisco with Oakland, Berkeley, and Alameda, is by far the longest bridge in the world and presented other problems never solved before. The Brooklyn Bridge, long the world's largest, would not stretch one-fifth the distance across San Francisco Bay. The Sacramento River had for centuries been carrying silt into the bay, till there was a cushion of it one hundred feet deep, yet the water still was more than one hundred feet deep. The engineers created steel tubes so large they could operate "clamshell buckets" in them. A clamshell bucket is a kind of scoop which will plunge down and come up with huge bites of mud. The bottoms of the steel tubes had cutting edges. A cluster of them, with concrete between them, was sunk to the mud. Their great weight made them sink into the mud, the clamshell buckets scooped it out, and that went on till the tubes were down to bedrock. Thus each cluster of steel tubes, with concrete around them, became a reinforced concrete pillar, and when the tubes were filled with concrete the pillar was tied into bedrock.

By that method engineers could build a cantilever bridge from Oakland to Yerba Buena Island, but from the island to San Francisco was still twice as far as across the Golden Gate. The engineers had to find a place midway in the bay where they could build a giant tower, which would be the joining point for two suspension bridges in tandem, or so arranged that the vast weight of one would pull against or balance the weight of the other.

Most big bridges have only five or six piers. The Bay Bridge has fifty-one. The bridge is double-decked, the lower deck being for street cars and truck traffic. The bottom of the bridge is 218 feet above high tide. Including its approaches and the biggest-bore tunnel in the world on the island, through which the double-decked bridge passes, the bridge is more than eight miles long, and more than four miles of it is over water.

When it comes to tackling the impossible, though, can anything quite equal pushing back the ocean tides and making a river run uphill?

The Sacramento River is one of the country's worst when it is bad. Like the Mississippi, it has levees along it. It likes to break out of its banks and flood a million acres of the most productive farm land in the world. At other times it pines away, so that when high tide sweeps through the Golden Gate even the great breadth of San Francisco Bay doesn't satisfy it, and it runs ninety-eight miles up the Sacramento River to Sacramento. That would be all right if the salt water didn't seep into

the soil along the way, worrying those who produce 95 per cent of all the canned asparagus for
this country, for one thing, and quite a lot of other
table delicacies.

What the Sacramento River did in the Sacramento Valley was almost paralleled by what the
San Joaquin River did in the San Joaquin Valley,
which really is the southern end of the Sacramento
Valley. The San Joaquin River rises in the High
Sierra and used to be navigable from Stockton to
points 150 miles inland. Now so much of its water
is used by ranches past which it meanders that the
western end of it almost dries up in summer, and
many of the ranches dry up, too. There are areas
of little rain in which once flourishing orchards
have become skeleton trees. Yet winter rains and
melting snows in spring often make the San
Joaquin dangerous and destructive.

Some persons might say that was the will of God
and the law of nature, nature's established custom
for untold centuries. California's public-works engineers decided it was the will of God that men
should use their heads to make nature serve them,
and that the drought and flood problems were all
one. Below Mount Shasta more than one hundred
inches of rain might fall in a year, in some parts
of the San Joaquin Valley less than five inches.
Those points might be seven hundred miles apart,

but what of it? By building a great flood-control and power dam below Mount Shasta, they could create a lake covering close to seven thousand square miles and turn Shasta's tremendous rainfall into money in the bank, to be drawn on as needed. Every day they could use enough of it to supply all northeast California with electricity. In summer what would have been winter or spring floods could be released in sufficient quantities to keep the Sacramento River high enough to meet the salt-water tides at the edge of San Francisco Bay and prevent them from rolling up the river. What was more, they could have water to spare to pump into a canal emptying into the San Joaquin River and make it navigable again, and to irrigate the thirsty lands of the lower San Joaquin Valley. That would, in effect, make the San Joaquin River run uphill. At least, the transfusion from the Sacramento would run uphill to stabilize its flow and give it strength. But the San Joaquin would help itself by learning self-control, too. A storage and power dam at Kennett would do that, turning its frenzied energy of flood times into controlled electrical energy and irrigation.

Thus the flood, drought, irrigation, and electrical problems of an entire state of more than 158,000 square miles—more than three times the size of New York State—have been taken into one comprehensive plan based on Hoover, Kennett, and Shasta dams, and San Francisco's astounding bridges are vital links not only in the state's transport system but in its economy. And nature doesn't seem to mind having California reverse its ancient laws that way. Instead, it seems to smile on California for making the most of what it has been offering to unseeing peoples through the centuries.

But still the headshakers and prophets of doom don't like it. At Shasta Dam last summer a woman visitor, watching the water tumbling down from a height much greater than that of Niagara Falls and creating more electrical energy than is produced on the American side of those falls, sighed:

"I don't think it's right to upset nature's plans that way. You can't tell me there's as much life in that water as there ought to be, after all that electricity's taken out of it!"

Ah, well! You can't please everybody. But most of us like California so well we can't help bragging about it unashamedly, as doubtless every reader has noticed. We are as proud of those who gamely failed as of those who won. We make heroes of the Donner Party, though there is evidence that some of them did shocking things. We make heroes of those who dared try to find their way through Death Valley, when that was a feat impossible to any wagon train. We are proud of Ralston the

Magnificent for what he tried to do, even though we smile at the great diamond hoax. We are proud of Serra and of Sutter, of Manly and of Burbank, of the way we have conquered time and space with airplanes, desert heat and mountain ice with air conditioning and snowplows, deserts with irrigation, floods with regulation.

We are proud of many "firsts" which have led our country and many other countries to progress, even including the first demand for an eight-hour work day, which was made in San Francisco in 1867, when most workers were on a ten- or twelve-hour schedule. We are even proud of our numerous crackpots and queer cultists and economists, because so often they give us something to laugh about. We are proud of all kinds of things, because it's an old California custom to be arrogantly proud of something, whether it justifies pride or not. But most of all we are proud of the California spirit, a thing which has been inspiring men to tackle the impossible ever since 1542, and to achieve it in a surprisingly high percentage of cases.